QUES
for UNITY

with Silver Voice and the Trickster

KIRSTEN BOLWIG

To Walter.
From all the pieces
One Peace.
Kirsten x

StarDrum Books

First published in 2003 by StarDrum Books
ISBN 0-9544956-2-4
By arrangement with the author

A catalogue record for this book is available
from the British Library

Printed in England

StarDrum Books
PO Box 32 Lechlade GL7 3ZR England
books@stardrum.com
www.stardrum.com

In order for the Aboriginal community in Central Australia to develop at its own pace in this sensitive time, I have disguised the people and the place by altering all names. Furthermore, I have altered the names of the Aboriginal people of the Birri Nation to protect their privacy.

I have for the sake of maintaining narrative flow, taken the liberty of attributing to Annette some information that was in fact gleaned in a brief encounter elsewhere.

I dedicate this book to
my parents Bridget and Niels,
my sister Janet and
my beloved son Kieran.

I would like to thank all those who helped me on this journey, those who were supportive and those who challenged me to grow.

Particularly, I would like to thank the presidents of Creative Health Network Suzanne Keehn and Pamela Perry, Madonna Ministry Bishops Charlie Sommer and Mei Lan Willis, Roy Little Sun, Mandi and Nancy Attinger, Carlo Hawkwalker Carlino, Tom Nasan, Magaer Lennox, Heidi Lex and Lynette James.

I would like to also thank Sue Smyth for her sterling work in editing.

CONTENTS

Coyote The Trickster is a character found in Native American Spirituality/mythology. He teaches that wisdom can be learned through the mistakes that are made. His antics are often comic and absurd. The Trickster features in the spirituality of many indigenous people but interestingly, rarely in this form of teacher in Aboriginal mythology.

AUTHOR'S NOTE

This is a time of extraordinary change. Things are happening to ordinary people that are mind-expanding and life-changing. I pride myself on being a person of sound common sense, with my feet planted firmly on the ground. I have a horror of being considered 'away with the fairies', 'a space cadet'. Yet this book contains many events that people might dismiss as the product of an overheated imagination.

I have a good, creative imagination, that is true, and it may have some bearing on my openness to some of the experiences I have had. But everything that is in this story is true: the events described, witnessed by others as well as me and in the case of the axe, more than twenty others.

I come from a background in education. My father is a scientist, a zoologist, and I grew up in an atmosphere of research, where theories were tested thoroughly, where proof was what mattered. Through my mother I gained an interest in the spiritual side of life. Through them both I gained my belief in the equality of all people. Both of them, particularly my mother, were active in civil rights in South Africa before it became The Republic of South Africa. I started my life more at home with my African companions than with white people. Together we romped amongst the blue gum trees of Windsor Woods outside Johannesburg. It was a happy time and yet I was very aware of the prejudice and hatred of white people towards black people. I was witness to terrible events. Victims of stabbing and beatings often found their way to our door. It was well known by all around that we would help.

When I was eight, a photographic exhibition came to Johannesburg called 'The Family of Man', which had a powerful impact on me. The catalogue from the exhibition is one of the few possessions I still have from my childhood. Many of the quotations I have used in this book were used in that exhibition and are my way of paying homage to it.

I lived in South Africa until I was ten, when events forced us to leave in 1958. We moved first to Uganda and, following that, to Nigeria. For a time I boarded at Sidcot, a Quaker school in Somerset, and it was there that I became familiar with the practice of meditation in the Sunday morning meetings. Quaker religious thought on 'the God within' was a powerful influence on my thinking.

When the International School was built in Ibadan, I went back to Nigeria to school and was there for both the first and second coups, witnessing violence and bloodshed as intertribal hatred flared. Leaving at the outbreak of the second coup, I returned to England to become a teacher. I think I have always had a profound awareness of and love for God but it does not find expression within orthodox religion or any other spiritual system. It is a deeply personal experience that evolved as a child out of solitary walks and play in the African bush. Sir George Trevelyan's words, "We are all droplets in the ocean of God", aptly describe how I experience this All Powerful, All Creative Source of my being. My openness to the ceremonial work of Native American Indians originated with an art diploma dissertation titled 'My hands are the tools of my soul', on the spirituality expressed within the arts and crafts of Mid-western tribes.

My current interest in personal growth and spirituality emerged in my late twenties and by the time I reached my mid-thirties I had left full-time teaching to become a healer and therapist. This continues to be my main work today, but with the many things happening in my life right now, I do wonder for how much longer this will be.

There is a river flowing now very fast.
It is so great and swift, that there are those who
will be afraid. They will try to hold on to the shore.
They will feel they are being torn apart and
will suffer greatly. Know the river has its destination.
The elders say that we must let go of the shore,
push off into the middle of the river,
keep our eyes open and our heads above water.
And I say, see who is in there with you and celebrate.

At this time in history, we are to take nothing personally.
Least of all ourselves. For the moment we do,
our spiritual growth and journey comes to a halt.

The time for the lone wolf is over.
Gather yourselves! Banish the word struggle
from your attitude and your vocabulary.
All that we do now must be done
in a sacred manner and in celebration.

WE ARE THE ONES WE'VE BEEN WAITING FOR.
Oraibi - Arizona

PROLOGUE

In this period of humanity's history, an increasing number of us are becoming aware of meaningful synchronous events occurring in our lives and are open to being guided by them, seeing them as neon lighted signposts highlighting the way most perfect for us as we travel through life.

This book is about just such a journey. But what started off as a trail of self-discovery carried me beyond myself. The psychological and spiritual journey towards personal wholeness transformed into a quest which took me to the other side of the world in search of a place and the group of people who lived there.

For me it was the starting point of connecting with the knowledge of an ancient people who retain the understanding of how to live in tune with the Earth. All I had to go on were the instructions of a mystical voice and a series of visions.

The adventure, which is still unfolding, started like this......

CHAPTER ONE

"With all beings and all things we shall be as relatives."
Sioux Indian

"We shall be one person."
Pueblo

*"It is time for humanity to return to the Self-Enforcing
One Law of the Infinite Universe....."*
Roy Little Sun

March 4th 2000.

I glanced at the clock. Only ten minutes to starting time. There was no way I could possibly make the distance of twenty miles from Bath to a rendezvous point in Avonmouth. Besides, I would have to cross Bristol, one of England's busiest cities in Saturday morning traffic to get there.

But something was impelling me to try. For some reason it was important that I should join the group. I was being prompted by the same instinct that three years before had urged me to attend the Healing Summit where this story truly began.

I threw a prayer to the unseen realms to open the way for me to connect with the group and leapt into the car, thus starting a chain of extraordinary events and synchronicities that would eventually lead me to a place called Unity in the outback of Australia.

I sped through traffic lights without a hitch, traffic jams miraculously opened out to clear a way and a sense of conviction bordering on euphoria developed. I knew without doubt that I would connect with the group. I thought about the purpose of the day, 'Healing the African Wound.'

Much of Bristol's early wealth from sugar and tobacco was built on the back of the slave trade. Echoes of the old abuse trapped in the city fabric has fed uneasy race relations, with negativity that flares from time to time into open hostility and trouble in the area of St. Pauls. The day was going to take the form of focused healing intent round a ceremonially created medicine wheel based in Native American tradition but of Roy Little Sun's own devising. The intention was to release this abusive energy and the anger it had generated.

Medicine Wheel

Roy Little Sun, an adopted Hopi elder, has committed his life to the re-establishment of world harmony. Some years ago, he had a vision of a peace ceremony the purpose of which was releasing trapped negative memories locked within land. The 'Circles of Hearts', medicine wheels created from one hundred and eight stones, have esoteric significance. Their construction by all present plays an important part in focusing the love and the healing intent in every ceremony. Several times in the past I had helped in the creation of one of these medicine wheels, seeing groups of disparate people being drawn together over the course of a day until hearts and minds resonated as One. Such was the power of Love that emanated from the sacred space created.

I was reflecting on my involvement in Roy's ceremonial peace work, when I arrived at Avonmouth station thirty-five minutes late. Nevertheless I was in time to see a cavalcade of cars leaving the car park and, in the back of one, I spotted the slight figure of Roy Little Sun. I tagged onto the end, thinking how beautifully the Universe supports us when something is meant to be. Driving along at the rear, I continued my reflections.

I met Roy at The 1998 Creative Health Network Summit, held at Millfield School in Street, near Glastonbury. This unassuming man, who stayed quietly in the background, impressed me as he spoke of his mission to heal the rift between the black and white races. Like many others, I was aware of the immense loving healing power that radiated from the medicine wheel he had created in the central hall. My ongoing involvement with him has resulted in experiences that many would say were miraculous but on this particular day I was about to have an experience in front of a great many witnesses that was to impact upon us all.

The convoy turned off the main road and followed signs to Severn Beach. Situated as it was at the mouth of the River Severn, up which all the ships carrying cargo and slaves sailed to reach Bristol Docks, I could appreciate why it had been decided upon as the place for the 'Circle of Hearts' Ceremony. The first cars finally drew up and parked. Roy eased himself out of a packed car. He stood talking to another person while tugging absentmindedly at his goatee beard. His preoccupied expression cleared as he spotted me. "Ah, Kirsten! Welcome!" he exclaimed and he came over to embrace me. We had not seen each other since a gathering in Snowdonia, the previous summer. Together we walked to the beach, catching up briefly on events as we went.

As I caught sight of the beach, my heart sank in dismay. The word 'beach' was a joke. The place was a solid sea of dank, stagnant-smelling mud stretching drearily along the shoreline. An upended shopping trolley with buckled wheels and festooned with the tattered remnants of a plastic bag stuck forlornly out of its grave of sticky mud. Unidentifiable mechanical parts, the bedraggled remains of a large dead bird, discarded bottles and tins scattered its length - cast-offs of both sea and humanity. In the grey gloom of that cold March morning, it looked absolutely dismal. I pulled my collar up and thrust my hands deep into my pockets as I hunched over trying to expose as little of myself as possible to the torments of the spiteful breeze.

Roy, seemingly oblivious to discomfort and undeterred by the unpromising environment, instructed us about the task of collecting stones for the medicine wheel. We were to look, he said, for stones the size of a large hand, which were shaped like Africa.

"And find a special stone to mark the day for yourself," he added as a seeming afterthought.

Eyeing the mud, I thought it highly unlikely we would find one hundred and eight Africa shaped stones, let alone a special one. But in that I was wrong.

Tramping along the mud-line, my eyes glued on the ground, I suddenly spotted an object that sent, for a few brief moments, shockwaves coursing through my body. What appeared to be a grey and mummified finger was protruding from the mud. A well-defined fingernail and wrinkled knuckles were clearly visible. I stared down at it in a long moment of apprehension, then with huge relief I realized it was only a stone and stooped to pick it up.

Imagine the effect on me when, as I did so, I heard a clear, strong voice in my head saying, "Follow the pointing finger. It will lead you to your special stone." Extremely startled, I followed the instruction immediately and without questioning. Sod's Law was operating in full force. The finger pointed out across the mud. Within a few short steps I found myself floundering ankle deep, each footstep taking me into deeper and deeper mud. With loud, sticky sounds it tried to suck the shoes from my feet as I struggled to keep my balance. This was madness!

I tried to turn back, strongly assailed by doubts about the wisdom of following a disembodied voice so blindly, but as I did I heard the voice again. It repeated the instruction as clearly and as strongly as before. My heart beat faster. Something very strange was happening. I resumed my slipping, sludging progress onward through the mud, each footstep squelching in a loud accompaniment. To boost my courage, I began to mutter the instruction out loud, repeating the words like a mantra. Then began to sing: "Follow the pointing finger" to the tune of "Follow the yellow brick road." Other stone gatherers looked up from their muddy search in amused incomprehension. Mad woman, they must have thought.

Severn Beach

The distance I walked was, I estimate, comparable to a circuit of a stadium running track. I was close to a curious mound of earth topped with sedge-grass, when the voice suddenly spoke again saying, "Stop! This is it."

At my feet was a slight mound, the bulge indicating the presence of a stone buried in the mud. It was impossible to see the shape or to know its size. Drawn to it, I began to scoop the mud aside, forcing my fingers deep into the sticky, foul smelling clay to release it. Clay sucked at my hands and great gobbets stuck messily to my fingers making the task slower and more arduous than I expected. I was conscious as I did so of a parade of images floating through my mind. I saw African Bushmen around their night-time fires under the African skies, but after a while it changed and I became aware of an Australian Aboriginal man in dark silhouette.

I registered this, for I already had plans set in motion for attending the Australian Healing Summit 2000 in August. "Now, there is a wound that needs healing," I thought to myself. "Work needs to be done for them, too."

With those thoughts and images in my mind, I lifted the stone clear.

It was a surprisingly heavy stone about eight inches long. Even through its clinging layer of mud, I could see that I held in my hands something quite remarkable. I looked around and found a shallow puddle of water caught in a depression in the mud. With careful fingers I rinsed it, revealing a thing of extraordinary beauty. Curved at one end, it tapered to a blunt point at the other. It had two faces. One face of the stone was pale in colour, the other dark and shiny. Light and dark came together along a cutting edge. In my hands was a beautifully fashioned, perfect axe, later to be identified by archaeologists as Neolithic and at least six thousand years old.

As I stared at it, I felt the most exquisite sense of joy, relief and home coming surging through me. It felt almost as if this was a long lost and treasured belonging being re-found. Strongest of all the feelings I experienced was that of completeness, a coming into wholeness and being very 'earthed'.

I tilted the axe back and forth to examine its beautifully mottled granular surface and fancied I saw faces appearing and disappearing within the markings. One face kept reappearing when the axe was tilted in a certain way: the venerable and wise old face of a man with a flowing beard, his face serene and eyes closed in meditative repose. I fancied he must be the spirit of the stone.

I could sense ancient memories held in the crystalline structure, hidden wisdom locked within. Its form perfectly symbolized the union of opposites, a concept that had been dominating my focus for some time. For me, it demonstrated clearly the times and experiences through which we are living: how we are learning to live with and embrace the paradoxes in life, accepting them without judgement; how we are all being called to return to our wholeness, everything, in all its diversity, an integral part of the Whole.

Within its shape it contained all. One end was rounded and feminine, and the other tapered to a masculine point. Its gracefully curved surface was honed at one end

into a sharply incisive cutting edge. One face was light and the other, dark. All opposites brought together within the whole to create a thing of great beauty.

I stood there for so long that I attracted the attention of others. One by one they drifted over to see what I had found. All were awed by it. It had a powerful presence. Energy seemed to emanate from it.

Throughout the day everyone's attention kept returning to the axe. Roy used it as the basis of his teaching about returning to Oneness. Dark on one side, lighter on the other, with both colours meeting on the cutting edge, it became the symbol for the day - healing the rift between the black and white races.

"What are you going to do with it?" everyone asked. "I am going to take it to Australia, to meet with the Aboriginal people," was my spontaneous reply. I looked down on the medicine wheel we had created between us. I told them of what I had been thinking as I dug out the axe.

"I would like to take it to Uluru, to the Keepers of the Rock," I added. "I feel I will learn something there, maybe linked with healing the Aboriginal wound." And with that statement, I set the course for a journey to a distant land, one that would be filled with amazing experiences that would lead over time to greater maturity of understanding.

Leaving the medicine wheel to decorate the dreary landscape, we drove back towards the city. The day was completed in the old harbour area of central Bristol. As the sun set on the chilly March day we stood in a circle and silently sent thoughts of peace out to the area. We focused on forgiveness and healing for the past, and the release of all the negative memories stored in the fabric of the city, of greed and exploitation past and present.

Then quietly we broke up and went our separate ways. As I turned away, I realized I was shivering with cold. A need for warmth dictated my next move. Following some of the others, I went into the Arnolfini Gallery café that stood overlooking the harbour. The fuggy atmosphere of heaving, noisy humanity was almost too much of a contrast, but the beckoning smell of express coffee enticed me. Glancing up I froze, my cup midway to my lips, my eyes drawn to the current exhibition. There in front of me was a large Aboriginal painting. It was part of an exhibition by an Aboriginal artist. I wandered round the exhibition deeply affected by what I saw. The paintings were powerful statements on the deep pain and suffering caused to his people by white settlers in Australia, and by the continual lack of both understanding and recognition of their perspective on life. However, it was the final picture that for me had the greatest impact. It was an image of an Aboriginal man looming out of the night sky.

****

CHAPTER TWO

"Carry your colours with honour on the trails of life.
Answer the cry within."
Song of the Circle. Barry Brailsford

"A few people joined together and thinking deeply
will do more to affect the conditions of the world than
millions of people joined in superficial thought.
That is because the morphic resonance of loving thought
is a literal forcefield, not just a metaphorical concept.
It is the sahimsa of which Gandhi spoke, carrying
within itself more potential power than any nuclear
bomb or military force. The question for our time is
whether enough of us are prepared to harness that power
for the purpose of national and planetary healing."
Marianne Williamson

Looking at the painting, I realized that this was the beginning of another chapter in an already unfolding adventure, one that I had embarked upon three years before, in the early spring of 1997.

Throughout March and April I had been eyeing an application form for the combined World Federation of Healing and Creative Health Network Healing Summit to be held in Monterey, California.

In the information pamphlet I had read that Creative Health Network "served an international community of people who take an active interest in what can be called 'creative health'." I was impressed by its inclusive vision of world community.

This was the type of organization for which I had long been searching. With the approach of the new century and Mother Earth moving relentlessly forward in her own evolution, I had been feeling increasingly frustrated by the mess civilization was creating in the world - not just in a few places but globally. Now I was being offered an opportunity to join a group of people committed to creating a healthier world to leave future generations.

Yet despite being so interested, I was reluctant to commit the huge amount of money involved. The application form had shifted from the top of one 'pending attention' pile of papers to another as I sorted. It nagged at me. It almost bleeped at me. But I had done nothing but look and wonder until Rosemary, a friend, announced that she had signed up.

Wasn't I going? She asked me.

That decided me. Rosemary and I joined forces for the Summit and it was an amiable partnership for the length of time it lasted.

****

The evening before we left, I quietly tuned in to the journey I was about to take. This was an opportunity for like-minded people to work together to create a global community but what opportunities would arise for me personally?

I closed my eyes and gradually became aware of a parade of North American Indian faces, each one replacing the last like a moving portfolio of sepia coloured photographs showing the Indian Nations. I understood this to mean that American Indians would somehow figure prominently in my experience. My interfering mind kicked in and began to plan.

I thought of ways I might get to New Mexico and who to approach to gain an introduction to members of the Hopi Nation. The Hopis held a fascination for me that had been with me since the seventies when an art dissertation, 'My hands are the tools of my soul', took me into the archives of the Victoria and Albert Museum to research the interconnectedness of art and spirituality for the Midwestern Indian Nations. There I discovered several fascinating books about the Hopi ways and one about wisdom stories of a Hopi Grandmother. The names of these books have long been forgotten but not the impact made on me, or the yearning for more that they left me with.

As I sat there thinking, I became aware that I was receiving a strong impression about what the journey would mean for me. It was as if a silent voice was speaking within, flowing into my consciousness on a wavelength of silver. For most of my life this 'Silver Voice' has 'spoken' to me and guided me at important times.
The message I was getting was intriguing. I understood that, during my time in the USA, I would find three Places of Power. There I would become "earthed" in a new and powerful way. This would form my "bridge to the sky", enabling me to bring my dreams more easily and potently into manifestation.

The silent voice spoke of a place of power by the sea. I had to assume this was Monterey itself. Another place was in the mountains. As I intended to revisit the

Yosemite National Park, I took it for granted this would also be the second place of power. Suddenly the word "Esselen" popped into my head accompanied by an image of soaking in hot bubbling water under a full moon and the stars. This would be the third place of power. I assumed this to be The Esselen Institute, a centre for self-growth, situated on the old coastal road south of Monterey. In the grounds of the Institute I had heard there were natural hot springs, which, as an outsider, one could visit between midnight and three a.m. So a trip to the Institute at the time of the full moon also got drawn into my plans as an absolute 'must do'.

How wrong I was in my assumptions. Everything took place exactly as the voice described but apart from being right about Monterey, the other situations were totally different from what I had envisaged and twice as thrilling.

CHAPTER THREE

*"The ideal world that transcenders see so easily
and so vividly is easily obtainable."*
Maslow

"Nothing great was ever achieved without enthusiasm."
Ralph Waldo Emerson

"The Universe resounds with the joyful cry 'I AM'."
Scriabin

Rosemary and I arrived two days before the Summit in San Francisco on the evening of October 8th 1997. Rosemary's energy was irrepressible and often left me feeling breathless. She approaches everything in life with huge enthusiasm. A natural organizer, she determined to make the most of her time there. Having done a lot of research beforehand, she knew exactly what she wanted to see. She made it perfectly clear that she was not prepared to negotiate over the sightseeing itinerary. Having been there before, this did not bother me. I was content to follow her lead.

Everything that happened was perfect preparation for the week ahead. Zipping our jackets against the fresh San Franciscan breeze, we rode a tram next day to the top of Nobb Hill, to get a view of the city. As it rattled its way up the steep incline, we savoured the novelty of this antique form of transport. It was a handsome vehicle with well-polished wooden panels, ornate brass plates and windows open to the elements. The atmosphere on board, although crowded, was good-humoured.

Even the locals smiled and cracked jokes with the tourists. It was a startling contrast to the fixed gazes and dour expressions seen on the London Underground. What impressed me most was the San Franciscans' unerring skill in leaping aboard the moving tram, fingers and feet miraculously finding secure purchase on the small crowded entry platform, and off again without checking their stride, as they continued about their business. As the rattling tram clanged its way to the top of the long hill, we realized that our choice to ride had been wise, for it meant that we alighted feeling fresh beside Grace Cathedral. It loomed over us, from across the street, a large, unattractive modern building. But once inside, I was struck by a great sense of peace and expectation.

An organ rehearsal was in progress. It was an exhilarating experience standing behind the organist, watching him struggle to master the difficult hand and foot work, listening whilst his effort was translated into soaring notes which reverberated round the cathedral in quadraphonic sound.

Looking past the organist down the nave towards the entrance, I noticed a group of people intently walking back and forth. I wandered over, intrigued to find out what they were doing, and discovered they were walking a replica of the huge labyrinth at Chartres Cathedral. I felt a leap within me as I recognized this to be a significant moment. Labyrinths and their use as a spiritual tool interested me. I stood for a moment in silent debate. Should I or should I not join in? It would enable me to spiritually cleanse myself like others before me.

I made my decision. I followed the winding course, intentionally letting go of the past and all that no longer served me, opening myself up in readiness for what was to come. In the meditative silence I felt a connection with Creative Intelligence infinitely greater than myself. A surge of joy flooded through me that stayed with me right through to the opening ceremony of the Healing Summit in Monterey.

The Monterey Beach Hotel, where we were staying, was situated in the most stunning water's edge position looking across the Bay to Monterey and Carmel. As they arrived, singly and in groups, the delegates gathered outside on the beach. They stood against a backdrop of Pacific rollers that crashed onto the beach and swept up the sand almost to the base of the hotel building.

Then, hand in hand, along the winding path of a labyrinth created in sand, over two hundred people walked together, away from the old order and into the new.

****

Feeling heady with the power of the moment, I was reluctant to join with the others when they went into the conference hall for the opening presentations. I stayed instead on the beach, conscious of wanting to be surrounded by the four elements. Alone, I sat down on the sand and went through an earthing exercise. Imagining a source of Power and Light above my head I breathed it in through the crown and out through the soles of my feet into the earth. I then reversed the process.

The effect was the strongest power charge I had ever felt. I had the sensation of being thrown backwards, like a formula-one driver revving away from the starting pad, by a force accelerating through me. The energy in my legs shot through the soles of my feet like two oil-boring rods plunging into the earth with real vigour. An explosion of colour filled my vision. I looked around, viewing the world in magenta - sand, sea, sky and people. Just as I feared that I might somehow have damaged my eyes, my vision cleared and I saw a spectrum instead: vivid red, intense orange and deep yellow, followed by softer more subtle greens, blue-greens, blues and violets. It was breathtaking and, most significantly, inverted.

My "bridge to the sky" was formed in that moment. In apparent acknowledgment of what was happening, I spotted a school of dolphins playing out at sea.

And beyond them, across The Bay, John Denver lost his life as his plane crashed into the sea off the headland called Lover's Point.

****

Next day I attended a workshop called "In Sound and Harmony". My interest flared when the leader spoke of her background. For some time she had worked with dolphins in the Mediterranean, taking groups of ill and handicapped children to meet them. She was emphatic in her belief that these visits were healing for the children. Watching them play and listening to them communicate with each other through clicks and whistles had a noticeably beneficial effect on the children. She was certain in her belief that the sounds held healing benefits for the human energy field. Since we were by the sea she said, it was appropriate to start the afternoon with the meditation she used for calling dolphins. Relaxing, eyes closed, we listened to her as she prepared us for the exercise. Starting with a long low sound and gradually rising up the scale, she invited us to focus on the seven main energy centres of our bodies. (In Eastern Spiritual systems, these centres of energy govern every aspect of the human experience.)

Her voice, powerful and penetrating, filled my body with vibrating sound until I felt dissolved in it. By the time she reached the final centre, the crown, I felt expanded, in an altered state though still able to hear her voice floating across an ocean of distance. Tuning in to dolphin energy, eyes still closed, we invited them to join us. Very soon I started receiving strong mental images of swimming with dolphins, spiralling in a vertical underwater ballet, hearing the clicks and whistles very clearly in my imagination as I called to them. I felt sure they would come, yet when they came, not ten minutes later, I was deeply affected. Tears coursed down my cheeks. In this heart-opening moment I experienced an unbelievable

range of deep emotions. I felt exquisite joy yet my heart ached with a deep, mysterious sadness and sense of loss. The dolphins - between sixteen and twenty of them - came surfing in on the waves closest to the shore so that we had a full body view of them. They planed through the water in groups of four, like jets in an aerial display, peeling off to the sides in the nick of time before beaching themselves.

Instinctively, the group felt the need to respond to this wonderful display. It felt quite natural that we should use sound. As one, we trooped out onto the balcony and sang to the dolphins until they left. When they had gone we stood and stared out to sea for a long time, each of us wrapped in silence, savouring the experience. Nothing else at the Summit could match this moment for impact.

It was a moment of great excitement for the hotel staff too. A receptionist told me that dolphins had not been seen close to the shore in The Bay for years. All evening, talk kept turning to their return.

****

The time at the summit was an extraordinary mixture of profound happenings - the dolphins' appearance; John Denver's plane crashing within sight of the hotel during the opening ceremony - and chaos.

Chaos because it was the first time a gathering of its kind had been attempted.

The call had gone out to people worldwide inviting them to come and contribute their talents, their expertise and wisdom free of charge. This was to be a gathering of peers, so everyone had to pay their own way.

And they did.

There were many wonderful people of great vision attending. We learned about previously unheard of projects; projects such as Bea Agins' work with the last known Shaman of the Achual Indians in the Peruvian Amazon jungle. Bea, a business woman, whose journey into the Amazon jungle had inspired her to change direction and become an anthropologist, was quietly recording the tribe's medicinal plants and icaros (spirit songs) needed for the healing rituals, doing this under the instruction of the dying shaman, Ramon. This small Californian woman had committed to holding this knowledge, sacred to the Achual Indians, until such a time as it could be handed on to an elected apprentice. At the summit, too, was Victor Beasley, an immensely tall, dignified black man whose charismatic presence matched his stature. He was a lion-hearted man with huge integrity, his commitment to world healing unquestionable. It was he who was largely responsible for organizing the drawing up of a manifesto for all with concern for the planet. Every day he closeted himself away with a group, working on the manifesto, until after intense discussion, The Healing Summit Agreement was condensed and distilled into six statements that spiritually inclined humanitarians the world over can use as their creed.

We acknowledge that all life on Earth
is created by Universal Intelligence,
and that our role is consciously to
cooperate with the Divine forces
of creation and compassion.

We agree to create, support and
implement that which unifies, balances
and heals the Planet Earth.

We support that which is required
for harmony to prevail within and
between all unique species, cultures,
races, and realms.

We as individuals,
commit to be true to that which we
hold most sacred in our hearts.

We, as a community,
commit to live our innate dynamic
vision of wholeness, mutual support,
and expansion of consciousness
for all beings.

We urge the application
of this agreement
in all human activity on Earth.

Later, copies of this Agreement were taken or sent to all the Heads of State, to the armed forces, religious and corporate bodies and others who play a key role in our planet's future. Periodically I wonder how many of them ever read it.

****

Rosemary and I made friends with Yosef, an Israeli member of the summit gathering. Yosef planned to visit the Yosemite National Park in a hired car after the Summit and felt it would be more enjoyable if done in company. This was a wonderful opportunity for Rosemary and me. Over a meal and a bottle of Californian wine, we made our plans together for the trip to Yosemite and it was agreed that Rosemary and I would head back to San Francisco to join him on the eastern outskirts a couple of days after the end of the conference. With eager anticipation I looked forward to whatever experience was waiting for me in the mountain wilderness.

However this was not to be. On the last evening, as we packed our bags in readiness for an early morning departure, Rosemary calmly announced she had made other arrangements for herself and would make her own way to the rendezvous point with Yosef. Staying alone in a youth hostel on Fisherman's Wharf in San Francisco did not appeal to me. The hurly burly energy of chaotic youth would, I knew, be difficult to handle straight from a gathering such as ours.

Indecisive, I started ringing around the local motels, and finding out about rail and coach connections to San Francisco's east side. I then ran into another problem. Yosef would not divulge the phone number of the brother with whom he would be staying. It was up to us, he said, to be at the rendezvous spot - and that was extremely vague - on time. He would leave without us if we were not there.

The sudden change in plans and the insubstantial nature of the arrangements made me feel insecure and angry.

But an alert part of me was also operating. I became aware that as this door seemed to be closing, something else must be about to take its place.

I was right.

Having failed to fix anything up for myself, I went to join the others on the beach for our final evening bar-b-que celebration.

Within half an hou,r an invitation to stay had been issued by a woman named Prudence, an imposing English Reiki Master and anthroposophist art teacher, whose regal bearing drew the eye. For some years she had lived in Sebastapol, a Californian centre of anthroposophy and Rudolph Steiner education. A space would be found for my backpack and me in the car she was sharing she assured me, patting my hand.

However, she added, she was not going straight home.

"Evalena Rose and I are going to the Esselen Bear Clan ceremony first. You won't mind the detour, will you?" she said.

Esselen!

In a flash of insight, I knew that the Silver Voice had been referring to this Native American tribe.

CHAPTER FOUR

"Never doubt that a small group of thoughtful,
committed citizens can change the world.
Indeed it is the only thing that ever has!"
Margaret Mead

"All are but parts of one stupendous Whole
Whose body Nature is, and God the soul."
An Essay on Man. Alexander Pope.

This was how I learned of the invitation from Tom Little Bear.

On its completion, a local member of CHN, Bruce, took a copy of the Healing Summit Agreement to Tom Little Bear, head of the local tribe, the Esselen, whose tribal grounds were in the Ventana Wilderness, a mountainous area flanking The Big Sur region of California. He came back with a wonderful invitation.

Having read The Agreement, Tom Little Bear was silent for a while. He recognized that we shared a common purpose. Obviously moved, he told Bruce about a Native American tribal gathering which was due to start on the day of our departure from Monterey. It was a meeting of Bear Clans, the healing clans, and they were gathering for the same purpose as our Summit.

As our summit drew to a close, so they opened in ceremony.

"The Bear Clans will be honoured," he said, "if as many of you as possible bring the energy of your Healing Summit to our opening ceremony."

And with this invitation the second part of my prophetic vision began to unfold, opening the way to the next bit of my journey.

I knew in that moment that, like a neon sign pointing the way, I was being shown what to do. Everything was right. Everything was just as it should be. My heart sang and insecurity fled.

I could have hugged Rosemary for her sudden change of decision.

****

The distance up to the sacred grounds was seventy miles. As we turned off the Carmel Valley Road, heading into the mountains, the way became narrow and twisting. The tarmac ran out and for the last fifteen miles we kept in close convoy up the dangerous narrow road full of hairpin bends and corrugations. How dangerous it was came to light after the ceremony when we were retracing our way back down.

The slopes were heavily wooded with California oak but through gaps in the trees we caught glimpses across deep blue-black valleys of the majestic mountain wilderness through which we were travelling. Occasionally we caught glimpses of the black, circling silhouettes of distant eagles as they rode the thermals in the intense blue sky overhead. In spite of the noise of the car engine, I was aware of the deep silence that surrounded us. Dark yellow dust broiled around us from the car travelling in front and I was thankful for the air conditioning that made it possible to drive with windows closed. Outside, the temperature was in the nineties, unseasonably warm. El Niño was wreaking its havoc along the California coast.

At last the convoy turned off the bumpy road - now not much more than a wide track - into a large clearing. Corral fencing surrounded the area, showing signs of human habitation but otherwise there was nothing to be seen but a large barn. One by one the cars were disgorged of people who held their tongues, allowing the silence to remain unbroken. Tumbled by a capricious breeze, a curled brown oak leaf scraped across the dusty ground, sounding quite deafening in the silence. Several minutes passed and then a figure appeared, walking between trees along a narrow footpath. Tom Little Bear beamed when he saw the largeness of the group gathered there.

Practicalities such as where to find the latrines were dealt with first. It was comical seeing relief on some of the older people's faces when they found that they weren't expected to squat behind a bush. Tom informed us that the Esselen tribe had formed a corporation called 'Window to the West', whose many activities fostered the renewed interest in this and other Native American Cultures and enabled outsiders to experience the wilderness around Big Sur. Toilet blocks and running water had been laid on for the trail riders.

Regrouping, we listened to Tom Little Bear as he explained that we were about to enter sacred space. Right attitude and respectful conduct was requested. This ceremony was to mark a very special occasion. For years the Esselen had wanted to build a ceremonial roundhouse on their sacred grounds. Permission had been refused until council elders had deemed the tribe to be spiritually ready for the responsibility. Completed within the past four years and yet unused, the bringing of the Summit energy would be like a blessing on it for future councils.

Roundhouse

In single file, keeping our voices hushed, we entered the partially buried roundhouse, stooping as we walked through the funnel opening into the dim, dusty light of the interior. In the centre were four giant tree trunks holding up the roof, with a smoke hole in the middle providing the light. Circling the wall was a baked mud ledge providing the seating. With so many present, a great number of us had to sit on the packed earth floor; however, this ceased to bother me after a short time. I felt a pang of disappointment that there were so few Native Americans present. I soon realized that we were the first to arrive. To open the ceremony, Tom Little Bear told us a version of the wisdom story, The Four Directions. It went something like this -

In the beginning, the four races lived together. Then the Great Mystery sent each to take up residence at one of the four directions - the Black to the South, the Red to the West, the White to the North and the Yellow to the East. Each was made guardian of a precious spiritual gift. The Black Race of the South held the gift of child energy with its faith, trust and innocence. The Red Race of the West held the vision of the true goals and life's mission to be in harmony with Mother Earth and all her people - the two leggeds, the four leggeds, the winged ones, the stone people and the standing people (trees). To the Yellow Race of the East, the Great Mystery gave charge of inner silence and illumination and to the North, the White Race, It gave the gift of creativity, the intellect and wisdom. To the White Race the Great Mystery gave the additional charge of keeping safe the Sacred Hoop.

Over time, the creative intellect of the White Race began to work mischief. It was restless and bored. It took out the Sacred Hoop and looked at it. It turned it on its edge and so invented the wheel.

Using the wheel the White Race set off to the South to visit its brothers. The Black Race saw them coming and went out to greet them dancing in celebration, the rhythm of their stamping feet making the ground shake. When the White Race saw them, saw their youthful vigour and felt their rhythm, it became thoughtful. It wished to put all this vigour to good use. So it enslaved the Black Race and wheeled on to the East. When the Yellow Race saw them coming they went out to greet them. The White Race was intrigued by their serenity. The Yellow Race showed them how to connect with their own spirituality. Again the White Race's intellect interfered. They took spirituality and wrote it down, and with much misinterpretation, they created rigid doctrines that have made mischief ever since.

Then the White Race wheeled off to meet their Red Brothers of the West. The Red Race came out to greet them in great respect and shared with them their visions for living in harmony. Once again mind mischief occurred. The White Race wanted to capture the vision so it made a box for it and thus created television. The vision became tired and lifeless within the box. It lost its sense of purpose.

And so the Sacred Hoop was broken.

"But now," concluded Tom Little Bear, "the Great Mystery is working within the hearts of man to return the Sacred Hoop to its Wholeness."

Speaking in measured tones he paced around the central fire stopping at each direction of the compass in turn. He spoke of the visions of his people and the purpose of the Bear Clans' gathering. And all the while a young Indian man, a tribal dancer named Coyote The Trickster, softly beat his drum. The power began to build as Coyote broke into songs of gratitude and blessing. He called us to remember our roots, urging us to return to our own lands and reconnect with our own wisdom stories - the myths and legends of our own cultures.

"Respect our culture but respect your cultures too. May the people of your land find their own roots once more, for their hunger shows by them trying to adopt our ways," he finished.

He beat his drum. The power built and throbbed in the air as the dust motes glittered in the shafts of sunlight, and the smoke swirled through the hole in the roof.

Tom Little Bear then pulled out a cloth-wrapped object. Slowly and with reverent care, he unwrapped it and as he did, he spoke of 'walking our talk', about the importance of coming from our own integrity. When people sat in council, each person who spoke was required to hold the talking stick he said, revealing at last the talking stick of his tribe. He pointed to the black crow feathers bound to it at one end.

"These feathers are there to remind you to speak truly. They are there acting as witness to the truth of your statements. It is a sacred moment."

Holding the stick firmly in both hands, he bade each of us in turn to connect with our inner-self, then speak our vision and make a commitment in a statement of intention regarding our own part in world service.

Seventy people voiced their vision and their commitment in that sacred space, passing the talking stick from one to another.

With each statement the energy rose and gained power. The individual statements were having the effect of earthing the intention of the Summit itself in a way it had not been before. There was a feeling that something had shifted for the planet. In the verbalizing of our visions, we had created something that went out into the collective consciousness of humanity. I felt in that moment that peace on Earth was a real possibility.

As my turn came and I reached for the stick, I could hear my heart pounding as loudly as Coyote's drum. I was scared of the responsibility to which I was opening myself. I did not know what to say. A clear path had not yet opened up for me to follow. Grasping the stick tightly with both hands, I got to my feet and spoke of my gratitude for all the wonderful experiences opening up for me to be part of the movement for World Peace and Health, realizing as I did so how powerful was the desire for change at grass roots level. I committed to doing all in my power to help the planet and further the vision for world peace. Certainty filled me that it was not governments that would cause the change but ordinary people like those of us gathered in the roundhouse. Deep love and respect for the Earth Mother moved within me. I recognized I was in the process of developing a profound connection with her, an experience I wanted others to share.

Leaving the roundhouse, I savoured my newly awakened passion.

CHAPTER FIVE

*"We are called to walk beyond ourselves. To reach into the
realms of magic and dance the trails of the spirit."*
Song of the Circle. Barry Brailsford.

Travelling back down the mountain in the golden light of
late afternoon, the three of us were quiet, wrapped up
in our own thoughts, appreciating the unique privilege
we had been given. This mood of quiet was suddenly
shattered when out of the gloom we saw a figure running
up the road towards us. It was Bruce. He looked dazed
and disorientated as he leaned through the window to
speak to us. There had been an accident, he said. His car
had blown a tyre but simultaneously the engine had cut
out causing his brakes to fail and his steering lock.
Miraculously the road had straightened at that point and
a track leading up a gully opened dead ahead. Instead of
plunging down a hundred foot drop or into the rocky
mountainside, the car shot into the opening and fetched
up against a bank of earth with a hard jolt.

As we pulled up beside them, the shocked passengers
were still struggling to get out of the car, its bonnet half-
buried in a bank of earth. Only one, a woman, made no
attempt to move. She sat hunched over in the rear seat,
her face white with pain. Prudence, a trained nurse,
crawled in beside her and carried out a gentle
examination. She re-emerged a couple of minutes later
her face grim. The woman probably had a fractured rib,
she reported. It was plain that she needed hospital
treatment immediately. Here on the side of a mountain
in a remote spot there was no point trying to raise

emergency services. We would have to take her to hospital ourselves.

It was apparent that one passenger from our car would have to be left behind. Prudence was the only trained nurse amongst us so it made sense that she accompanied the woman to the hospital. With sinking heart, I volunteered to be the one.

As luck would have it, we had been invited earlier to overnight at the home of one of the conference contributors, Sophia, a singer-songwriter, who happened ⌐   ⌐d fortune, to live on the edge of the trir   ⌐ minutes drive further on down
                        ⌐ninutes later I stood, with luggage
              ⌐, gazing up at the rich red-brown walls of
        ⌐ɔen building nestling amongst trees against the ɔceep hillside. Once more I felt deeply insecure. I had been cast adrift. Yet here again there was also a feeling of alert excitement underlying the insecurity.

Sophia, a striking, big-boned woman with silver blond hair, came out on the wooden deck to greet me, and behind her padded three large dogs, one of which was pure white. As I struggled up the steep steps with my backpack, I realized with a shock these were not dogs, but wolves. They stood necks craning, tongues lolling, as they looked down on me with deeply penetrating gazes through the wooden bars. Like their human companion, I saw they were smiling. Sophia, holding open the fly screen door, gestured towards the other conference members being given houseroom for the night. Amongst them was Alyson, an English woman, with whom I had already struck up a friendship. I grinned at her, suddenly feeling reassured, and looked around for others who might be familiar. Leaning over the kitchen sink, long hair obscuring his face, stood another figure that I recognized from the roundhouse meeting. Crouching at his feet, a small pug, with jaws clamped possessively on his trouser leg, glared at all the strangers who had invaded his territory. Daniel brushed back his hair, leaving a silver streak of bubbles and raised a soapy hand in greeting. His self-appointed protector, Diesel, growled and munched furiously on his mouthful of material. It was several hours before Diesel relaxed his grip on the trousers, reassured at last that his beloved master was in no danger.

The evening passed, and one by one people drifted away to their beds until there were only four of us left talking quietly over cups of coffee.

Close to midnight, with the others asleep, Sophia suggested Alyson and I complete the evening with a soak in the outdoor hot tub situated higher up the hillside. Fainthearted at first, I refused, reluctant to brave the sharp night air but, finally persuaded, I climbed the hill and joined Alyson and Daniel already there, soaking in blissful contentment, two misty figures half hidden in steam.

At times talking, at times quiet, we relaxed together. As midnight passed Alyson and I fell silent, listening to wisdom stories told by Daniel, a traditional storyteller for the Cherokee Nation. Newly trained in his skill, he practised in preparation for a big powwow in Hopi Land. I began to understand the power in storytelling for imparting deeper truths and conveying concepts that are difficult to grasp. Listening, I knew that storytelling would become increasingly important in my life.

In the hot bubbling water, listening to Daniel weave the magic of those wisdom stories, I looked up at the beautiful glowing face of the full moon sailing like a queen across the heavens, surrounded by a vast entourage of stars. In the alchemy of moonlight, I fancied that the surrounding mountains were ancient giants, rocky shoulders hunching beneath shaggy cloaks of forest oak, as they leaned forward in listening silence.

Later, snuggled in a sleeping bag, I fell asleep listening to the gentle, snuffling breath of the three wolves while thinking of hot bubbling water under the full moon and the stars.

The last part of my prophetic vision had happened exactly as foretold.

Whatever followed during the rest of the trip, I knew it would not be as significant to my future as the events of the past week.

CHAPTER SIX

"Fools are like dogs.
When one starts to speak all the others join in,
And all who hear close their ears and turn away.

The wise man is like a cricket.
He waits for the silence then starts to sing.
And all who hear stop and listen."
Inner Guidance

"The land is a mother that never dies."
Maori

Through my experience in California in 1997, my respect for Native Americans had expanded into recognition of the hugely important role indigenous people round the world might play in the future in teaching the scientifically orientated consumer civilizations about love and respect for the planet and each other. Amongst these people struggling to hang on to tribal ways are the Earth Caretakers, keepers of ancient wisdom.

It was at the 1998 Healing Summit that Roy Little Sun made his appearance in my life. This, the second international summit, was held at Millfield School near Glastonbury.

Entering the conference hall for the first time, I was awed by the magnificent medicine wheel laid out on the floor below the stage, within its boundaries sacred objects placed with reverent care. The Circle of Hearts was Roy Little Sun's own creation, the hundred and eight stones creating it representing the completion of a cosmic cycle of consciousness. Roy was the adopted son of Grandfather Titus, a Hopi chief much revered for his wisdom. For many years he lived quietly together with Grandfather Titus on Titus Farm in Hopiland, Arizona. Some say Grandfather Titus was one hundred and twelve years old when he died. The great New Zealand story teller, Barry Brailsford, described him as being "old, yet timeless... One of the few great ones left." It was on Titus Farm that Roy first created his Circle of Hearts.

Roy, a slight, almost emaciated figure, his black hair winged with grey and scraped back into a pony tail, did not immediately draw one's attention. Yet when you looked at him you could see a quiet authority, and in his slenderness a wiry strength. It was when he spoke of his work that his presence began to make itself felt. This slight man became a giant.

He spoke first of The Prophecy Rock, a rock sacred to the Hopi people where an ancient pictogram depicts clearly the choice facing mankind at this present moment. He drew the pictogram. At the point marking the present time, it branched showing two clear choices: one, a route to destruction, the other, a route to living in harmony, peace and love.

Standing with quiet dignity beside the medicine wheel Roy explained its significance.

"Its purpose is to dissolve all fences that ultimately need to be defended with costly and cruel wars. In participating in the creation of this medicine wheel, individuals are signalling their belief that it is time for humanity to return to the Self-enforcing One Law of the Infinite Universe that freely and lovingly maintains all life. Every part of the medicine wheel has symbolic significance. Its creation is a conscious process. With the creation of Circles of Hearts around the world, global healing will also increase. Ultimately this will result in Mother Earth becoming One Medicine Wheel."

He spoke on, eagle feather in hand, his guttural accent making the words sometimes difficult to follow. But with my attention drawn constantly back to the medicine wheel, this did not seem to matter.

To one side of the hall another man, of a stockier build than Roy Little Sun, stood quietly listening, his hat brim shadowing his face, his long hair hanging loose over his shoulders. It was not until later that, emerging from the gloom of the hall into sunlight, I caught sight of him again. He had the strong and beautiful features of a Native American. Like Roy Little Sun, Carlo Hawkwalker Carlino, sun-dancer and pipe carrier for the Lakota Sioux, became a powerful influence in my life.

Throughout the conference I found myself gravitating towards these two men to listen to their teachings. We are all One. Everything is interconnected. Respect your Mother, each other, all life. Both he and Roy fed my growing awareness with a deep understanding of how vital it is for the people of the modern world to hear this message.

As I listened, I recognized that everything they taught I already knew instinctively and was already striving to convey to others - teachings about respect and integrity, about right action and attitude. Teachings about looking at the cycles and the natural order of things that will help us recognize our own cycles and the patterns of growth in our lives, about honouring this being called Mother Earth. But whereas the teachings of these two men were steeped in Tribal Law, my beliefs did not fall within any particular spiritual system. Everything I knew and believed came from within, from some source of inner wisdom. In a sense this imposed a handicap, for often I had no vocabulary with which to articulate this inner knowing.

Inspired by these two men, I felt prompted to repeat before ministers of an international church-without-walls the commitment I made in the Esselen tribal roundhouse in 1997. Standing beside a shaman from the Peruvian Huachuma tradition as he in turn made vows to uphold and spread the wisdom he had been taught, I felt tremendous peace. Love and joy flooded my heart. What I was doing felt right.

****

"The Great Sky Spirit told Crow that in reward for her sacrifice and service, her black feathers would reflect all the colors of Earth. Crow looked and saw thousands of tiny rainbows reflected in her feathers, and was happy again."
Lenape Legend

Wending my way back home after midnight on the last day, I listened to my sixteen year old son, Kieran, repeating stories he had heard from Carlo Hawkwalker. Clutched in his hand was a soft deerskin medicine pouch he had been given by Carlo as a parting gift.

"You will need to find some way to thank him for that," I observed.

Kieran thought a while.

"I will paint him a picture of the Rainbow Crow story," he said eventually and next morning, true to his word, he produced a simple, beautiful illustration of Rainbow Crow trailing a wonderful rainbow across the heavens.
Five days later I found a black feather on my doorstep. As I picked it up, all the colours of the rainbow shimmered across its beautiful surface.

Kieran's gift had been received.

****

"O wonderful,
Wonderful, and most wonderful wonderful!
And yet again most wonderful..."
William Shakespeare

Through the autumn of 1998, appreciation for this wonderful planet and Mother Nature continued to build. I was filled with an intense love of life. I found myself so moved by the beauty of nature I would feel tears coursing down my cheeks. It was an experience of gratitude so enormous that if the words 'Thank You' had been spelt out in giant capitals twice the size of those announcing 'Hollywood', it would not have been big enough. In love with Earth, I could not think of Her in any other terms than Beloved Mother.

Yet at the same time I felt restless. Living in Bath became uncomfortable, with all the concrete sidewalks separating me from contact with the earth. Living indoors became claustrophobic. I wanted all the windows and doors to be open continuously. Without the movement of air on my face, I felt I would suffocate. I longed to sleep out of doors in a tent to bring me into as close a contact with the earth as possible.

In this state of extreme sensitivity and awareness, my reflections turned, not for the first time, to how we in the Western World have a tendency to think of the Earth as an inanimate object there solely for the convenience of the human race, Nature being something to conquer and exploit.

But mankind is beginning to wise-up to the fact that we are not excluded from the Natural Law that governs all things. One by one our bubbles of superiority are being pricked as both ecological and man-made systems begin to collapse. Many changes are occurring around the world. Overnight the inconceivable becomes conceivable, as shown by the tearing down of the Berlin Wall.

People are turning to the internet to become better informed. Recycling initiatives, the fair trade movement and the steady growth in organic farming are quietly gaining momentum; subtle things overlooked in the strident clamouring of the media.

Encouraged by all this I felt very positive, arguing with pessimistic friends that there has to be breakdown of the old order before anything new can emerge, even if in our subjective judgement we cannot understand or be able to see the positive side to some of the things happening in the world right now.

On reflection, I could see that this held true in my own life, too. Through the breakdown of my marriage, new doors opened for me. As if in answer to my thoughts I opened a book and read:

> "All discord, harmony not understood;
> All partial evil, universal good."
> 'An Essay on Man'. Alexander Pope

CHAPTER SEVEN

"The universe will reward you for taking risks on its behalf."
Shakti Gawain

*"A discovery is said to be an accident meeting
a prepared mind."*
Albert Szent-Gyorghyi

This whole phase finally came to a head for me through an extraordinary event in Spain. It provided tangible proof of how responsive is Earth to our love and recognition of her. It added yet another strand to my understanding of the inter-connectedness of all things.

The companion with whom I travelled was a small woman, feisty by nature. I quickly realized that my highly exuberant energy was an overpowering irritant to her but found it difficult to curb. I knew that just as the crest of a wave cannot stay the crest forever, in its own time my euphoria would abate. In the meantime I saw no point in apologizing for it.

Our hosts, an English couple, met us at Alicante airport and drove us back to their home perched on the mountainside overlooking Oliva, a small Spanish resort on the eastern coast midway between Alicante and Valencia. Healers themselves, they had devoted their time to creating 'Sunflowers,' a peaceful spiritual retreat where busy people, in need of rest and nurturing, can go to recharge their batteries. Warm-hearted, kindly people, Vivien and Clive put a great deal of effort into making us feel relaxed and at home. They had adopted the Spanish attitude of 'everything in its own time' and this permeated the days as they slipped by.

Gradually things slowed, became timeless. Time suspended. The restless excitement eased into a more peaceful state of well being.

Roaming round the hillside garden, I was in touch with nature. Out of sight of the house, I found an old pine, its bark rough with age, resin tears weeping from old cracks. With my back against the trunk, I stared upwards through the knotted branches, watching buzzards. Crying plaintively, they wheeled overhead, their russet brown pinion feathers testing the thermals. Dreaming beneath the tree, I became aware of the billion moments floating in between the tick and tock of time.

Our mutual love for nature brought Vivien and I together during the first week and, scrambling down a slope on one of our walks, Vivien stopped and pointed to an area some distance away. It was a sandy red scar in the hillside, showing the telltale signs of excavation. Knowing I was interested in rocks and crystals Vivien said stones with white quartz deposits could be collected there.

Approaching it along an uneven boulder strewn path, we sidestepped down the final slope and onto the flat area of rich orange-red soil. I became aware that I was getting feelings of disquiet. Something was wrong. Distress hung in the air.

"Why do I feel distressed here?" I asked.

"It could be because there are plans afoot to build holiday homes over all this site."

"We must do something to try and protect this land," I exclaimed. I paused, thinking for a moment before suggesting we create one of Roy Little Son's Circles of Hearts both as protection and to restore harmony. The instant I said this, a glint of light from the ground in front of my feet caught my eye. It was so bright that I bent down to see what it was. I picked it up, and to my astonishment, found it was an absolutely perfect tiny double-terminated wand (a faceted crystal shaped like a wand, which is pointed at each end) of greenish brown crystal. I impulsively responded, "Thank you Mother. I am glad you are pleased by that."

Immediately there was another glint and once more I stooped to find another tiny crystal point, this time black. Vivien and I were very still. Something was happening. Surely this could not just be coincidence. The Earth seemed to be responding to what I said. We looked at each other then speaking simultaneously put it to the test. We expressed our feelings of being honoured and thanked the Earth.

"Mother Earth, I know you are communicating with us," I said.

Again there was a flash of light and again there was a tiny dark brown crystal, another double terminated wand. We knew now that there was no coincidence. The sense of honour was tremendous. As we once more verbalized our gratitude little lights began winking all around. It was as if a chorus of crystal voices clamoured, "I'm here! Take me too!"

Before our astonished eyes, as we looked on, crystals began appearing on the ground around our feet. Each time we expressed gratitude it seemed a fresh wave appeared. The realization that we were being showered with gifts was overpowering. My legs collapsed under me and I sank to the ground. On our knees we collected more than a hundred before I said, "We have enough. We must go and let you rest." But Earth had not finished. Her response was yet another wave of crystals. This time they were black clusters, like blackberries, and they circled my feet so that I stood in a ring of crystals, their points little prisms of sparkling light. We felt the strongest sense of Earth wanting to share herself, to communicate with us. We felt such love.

"Thank you," I breathed, picking up these beautiful gifts, "I will respond. I know you are asking for our help and I will respond."

Finally, overwhelmed by what was happening, we virtually fled, not feeling able to handle still further development. The unimaginable had happened. For me it demonstrated that the Earth is a sentient being, conscious of us, responsive to us and desirous of our recognition.

****

Back at 'Sunflowers' we sat for a couple of hours looking at the crystals, going over the events again and again, verifying for ourselves that it had happened. We counted one hundred and fifty crystals and shared them between us. Looking at these tiny crystals through a magnifying glass we were able to marvel at their perfection. Rainbows flickered off their tiny points. As we settled and were able to notice other things, we became aware of a sensation of peace and balance, pleasant relief from the mental and emotional chaos we had experienced such a short while before. The significance of this came much later.

I felt a deep sense of disappointment when our tale failed to impress Clive and my companion, Ruth. They did not appear to grasp the significance of what had happened.

I slid into depression, as low now as I had been high before. It was deepened by the knowledge that, affected by her husband's apparent disinterest, Vivien was no longer interested in creating the medicine wheel. I felt we had betrayed the Earth. We drifted apart, our closeness lost. I thought about creating a tiny medicine wheel out of the crystals I had, but I did not have enough and my estrangement from Vivien made me reluctant to ask her for some of hers.

Without telling anyone, I returned to the place. Alone, I cried and spoke aloud into the wind of my sense of failure and betrayal of trust. On my hands and knees once more, I scoured the sandy surface for crystal points to add to my number so that I could create the wheel. The Earth was unresponsive. No more crystals appeared. Sadly, I stood and prayed for protection for the land.

****

"And it is not always granted for the sower to see the harvest. All work that is worth anything is done in faith."
Albert Schweitzer

I was aware that the appearance of the crystals carried a message that I would have to share with others. Throughout the early months of 1999, I told the story and showed the crystals to all who would listen. If I did nothing else, I could act as messenger. I could share my belief that in restoring balance to our planet we can begin the process of restoring balance, harmony and peace to humanity. The crystals and the way they appeared were my proof.

I sought out gatherings where I was likely to be heard. Speaking so often about this wonderful sentient Being and her need for our help, I was in danger of becoming a bore to some and a pest to others.

I wanted to do more but had no ideas. I felt inadequate for any other task, being ill informed and ill equipped. I lacked the deeper wisdom needed. So I sought out those with greater knowledge who could shoulder the responsibility. Over the course of the year I gave away many of the crystals to people who would treat them with respect and use them with awareness. My collection diminished as crystals found their way into medicine pouches of shamanic healers from different parts of the world and into the hands of Elders connected with sacred lands, people who retain the knowledge of how to heal the land and maintain the balance.

About this time my path crossed those of Debbie and Eddie, a well-known couple of spiritual teachers, while staying at Little St Michael. The Glastonbury retreat adjoins the beautiful Chalice Well gardens, a haven of tranquillity for all seeking peace and replenishment. A special stillness permeates the place, a sort of timelessness where you expect to encounter faeries and elementals flitting through the bushes, and where you feel you can sit beneath a tree soaking up ancient wisdom.

Walking round the garden I was aware of this particular couple as they wandered back and forth along the paths, leaning forward to smell fragrant plants in passing. There was something about them that made me want to speak with them. My opportunity came in the evening. Debbie and Eddie were sitting at the kitchen table already eating when I went to prepare supper. We fell into conversation and inevitably I touched on my experience in Spain and all that had happened since. Showing them the crystals, I could see their delight as they marvelled at the exquisite perfection of the tiny faceted points. Yet, I felt an unaccustomed sense of caution when Eddie asked for a crystal to keep. I was confused. These were people for whom I felt instinctive liking. So why? Perhaps it was because their work had a different focus. I hesitated. At last, apologizing for my caution, I said that I would seek guidance through meditation.

In my room, curled up on my bed, I closed my eyes and tuned in to the crystals. Was it appropriate to give Eddie a crystal? Before long I heard the silent, silver voice speaking to me as it had done so many times before. Yes, it was appropriate, providing Eddie carried with him understanding of the purpose of the crystal. My interest quickened. This was the first time I had been told of a purpose. I had never actually formulated a question before about it.

I asked, "What is the purpose?"

There was a pause, then came, " I am a messenger of Union. I have no knowledge of separation. I hold the deep knowing of the rhythm and cycles and the natural pattern in all things. I come from the One Truth yet show you the multifaceted expression of the Whole."

I am a messenger of Union. I have no knowledge of separation. I hold the deep knowing of the rhythm and cycles and natural pattern in all things. I come from the One Truth yet show you the multifaceted expression of The Whole.

I hurried back to Eddie.

"Oh perfect!" He exclaimed when I told him, "Debbie and I are going to a border town between North and South Ireland. When I asked for the crystal I had it in mind to bury it there. Now I know why."

Ireland, a land of deep division, torn apart by conflicting ideologies.

I had given many crystals into the safe keeping of shamans and elders and now, reviewing where the other crystals had gone, I realized that they were all going to places of deep conflict or crisis. Places where people were massacring each other over differing beliefs. Places where people had lost their roots, driven out by hatred or greed.

It reminded me of the crystal I had given James Twyman some weeks before. I listened as The Peace Troubadour talked to a gathering of his experiences with Father John Alexis.

Father John Alexis is a man on a mission to plant six foot long peace poles wherever there is war. On the sides of each pole, written in their native tongues, are prayers for peace from all the major religions of the world. He believes that the poles, planted with his peaceful intention, act like acupuncture needles for the earth, helping to release from the area the blocked energies of hatred, fear and conflict. But he was in the midst of a dilemma. The devastating war in Kosovo was raging and authorities refused him entrance into the country.

His belief intrigued me.

Thus it was that when Jimmy travelled to Brazde refugee camp, on the border of Kosovo, he carried with him the most perfect of all my double terminated wands. It was buried there as a tiny acupuncture needle for the Earth, pulsating with its own message of peace. My heart felt painful as I handed it over because it was the first and therefore the most special of all those crystals for me.

Two weeks later there was an Easter Peace gathering near Glastonbury Tor. Seventy people stood in prayerful silence in the Chalice Well Gardens as Jimmy sang in Brazde. Listening to my intuition, I gave each person a crystal to hold. I did not understand the significance of what I had done until three months later.

As the sense of union built, the spirit of peace grew and flowed outwards from the gathered throng into the collective consciousness of mankind. Whether in truth this had any effect, it is a fact that a few days after the concert, television news reported a lessening of tension on the Kosovo border and the slow painful process of reuniting families began.

****

"Your desire is your prayer. Picture the fulfillment of your desire now and feel its reality and you will experience the joy of the answered prayer."
Dr. Joseph Murphy

In the summer of 1999, three months after the gathering in Chalice Well gardens, Carlo Hawkwalker returned to England for a gathering at the Royal Agricultural College in Cirencester. With pouch of crystals in hand I headed for the meeting. As before, his striking figure was prominent in the crowd. He stood to one side in quiet conversation, his dark eyes fixed on the person with him, a figure made familiar by the hat that never left his head and the black hair flowing over his shoulders.

Greeting me with a hug, he turned his attention to the crystals. I placed one in the palm of his proffered hand. He closed his eyes, a stillness descending over him. With gentle fingertips he rolled the crystal back and forth in silent communion with the stone people. At last he said, "These crystals are all of the same family. Wherever they are in the world they are in contact. They are acting as tiny transmitters, receivers and amplifiers for the message which they are sending forth."

CHAPTER EIGHT

"Be the change you wish to see in the world."
Gandhi

"Only after the last tree has been cut down
Only after the last river has been poisoned
Only after the last fish has been caught
Only then will you find out that money can't be eaten."
Cree Indian Prophecy

Bath looked beautiful from my hilltop vantage point. From there I could see houses usually hidden from view, nestling in unremembered valleys like Lyncombe Vale, valleys that remained like an open back door so that the countryside could sneak in to within half a mile of the city centre.

In the strong sunlight of a late summer afternoon, I leaned my back against a favourite tree and breathed in clean, fresh air, unpolluted by the traffic fumes that gathered in the city's bowl. Energy flowed in through my back and legs from the tree and the surroundings. This was where I often came to be recharged after a busy week. I called it my power tree. With energy restored, I could feel my feet once more firmly on the ground, my balance and ability to think clearly return.

It was sitting beneath this tree, writing in my journal, that my familiar silent voice once again flowed in on its wave of silver. Deep in thought at the time, it took a while to register.

A sentence popped into my head and I idly wrote it down. Then looking at the words, "Manifest your vision through a state of gratitude," I realised suddenly that the silver voice was once again speaking to me. Listening now, I wrote down the four statements that flowed into my mind.

"Gratitude is the most 'earthing' of states to be in. It profoundly connects us to Earth in a state of Love. It is a profoundly healing state for both the Earth and Humanity. When we are 'un-earthed' we cannot effectively manifest our dreams in the flowing way that is possible."

"Gratitude is the most 'earthing' of states to be in. It profoundly connects us to Earth in a state of Love. It is a profoundly healing state for both the Earth andHumanity. When we are 'un-earthed' we cannot effectively manifest our dreams in the flowing way that is possible." I realized the truth in the statements, particularly the last. After walks, things that had been eluding me suddenly met with success. Something was happening, without my being aware of it, every time I took a country stroll or spent some time in the garden, that was deeper and more profound than getting fresh air and exercise. I was being reconnected with Earth and through that, with my own internal rhythms.

Until this moment, I had been focusing on the message of union for the world, my attention on the macrocosm rather than the microcosm. Through this message on 'earth-ing', I was now being made to look at how the message applied to us as individuals. I thought deeply about the part of the crystals' message that said, "I hold the deep knowing of rhythms and cycles and the natural pattern in all things."

In my role as healer and a therapist dealing amongst other things with stress management, I had many people flooding to my door at this time. In a state of crisis, their lives in transition, everything familiar beginning to break down, they sat in the therapy room confused and anxious. Many were experiencing depression and fear over the chaos they saw around them in the world. Driven by bosses in the corporate world, they were out of touch with themselves and out of balance.

Confident of its importance for them, I encouraged my clients to develop an understanding of the rhythms, cycles and patterns in their lives.

I used the world of nature both in example and analogy to help understanding. Through it I was able to awaken insight that like the rest of nature, they too were governed by a rhythm of ebb and flow, their lives marked by fallow and fruitful periods. Within the little room we talked of being whole, not just as an individual or as part of the human race, but as part of everything.

Alongside my clients I worked on becoming a better caretaker for my own little bit of earth - my body - trying to become responsible by listening to and understanding its signals, recognizing and respecting its needs.

I became increasingly aware of being a cell in the planetary body, growing in understanding of the intricate interconnectedness of everything at ever- deeper levels.

By being a responsible caretaker for myself, I realized I was affecting everything else.

At this point, another synchronous event took place.

Nine months earlier, Bea Agins, my American anthropologist friend, had stayed with me during the '98 Summit using my study as her bedroom. After she had gone, the room remained undisturbed until one day an international psychic counsellor named David Cohen rang me to see if he could stay with me when he visited Bath. I was very doubtful. David has severe physical handicaps and I doubted strongly whether he could manage my stairs.

Using his mediumship to his advantage, he said persuasively, "My guide, Ishmael, says everything will be fine. There is no need for you to worry."

Unable to think of any further objections I agreed to a one-night trial.

I sighed as I surveyed the clutter of papers littering the guest room and started to clear them. My movements jogged the bed and there was a loud thud as something heavy fell to the floor. Whatever it was it had obviously been sandwiched between the bed and the wall. Lying across the bed, arm squeezed down into the gap, I felt around with my fingertips until they came across the flat hard shape of a book. On pulling it out I gave a gasp.

Its title was "Ishmael". What a coincidence!

On the back it read, "TEACHER SEEKS PUPIL. Must have an earnest desire to save the world. Apply in person."

Randomly opening the pages my eyes fell on a passage. I read:

"The people of your culture cling with fanatical tenacity to the specialness of man. They want desperately to perceive a vast gulf between man and the rest of creation. This mythology of human superiority justifies their doing whatever they please with the world, just as Hitler's mythology of Aryan superiority justified his doing whatever he pleased with Europe. But in the end this mythology is not deeply satisfying. The Takers are a profoundly lonely people. The world for them is enemy territory, and they live in it like an army of occupation, alienated and isolated by their extraordinary specialness."

Daniel Quinn's unique and captivating novel had arrived at just the right moment in my life. Like the critic from the Washington Post I was entrapped in the dialogue itself before I was half way through, wanting Ishmael, a talking gorilla, to teach me how to save the planet from humanity.

Its perspective on the hunter-gatherers and civilization made a deep impact on me. It supported many of the new ideas that were stirring in me and by the time I had finished reading it I believed many of my insights to be valid.

Although unaware of the outcome, I knew that a force was at work in my life which was steering me in a particular direction. All I had to do was keep on allowing myself to be guided.

CHAPTER NINE

*A problem cannot be solved at the
same level of consciousness that created it.*
Albert Einstein

My intention to go to Australia was not a spur of the moment decision made on a muddy beach on a miserable March morning. The holding of a Millennium Summit in Australia had been announced at the end of Summit '98. Although so far ahead, I made the commitment at that time to go. Something told me it would be very important. I was almost alone in this feeling. Many of my CHN friends felt the expense of the whole venture too great.

I remained confident in its importance, full of hope that this summit would demonstrate an evolution away from workshops and presentations towards a greater focus in using group energy for raising planetary consciousness.
In October 1999 Creative Health Network organized a 'think tank retreat' for a group of thirty people. The purpose would be to explore group dynamics and the purposeful use of group energy. The structure of the days and the subject of focus would arise out of group decision. This was a meeting of peers working together as peers. Armed with the crystals and the support of newly acquired insights from the book, "Ishmael", I headed for America.

Almost two years to the day, I was back in California standing uncertainly in the terminal of San Francisco airport. I looked around scanning the crowds. Before long I saw the familiar figure of Suzanne Keehn, president of CHN, hurrying towards me. "Oh there you are!" she exclaimed. "I have just been all the way to the wrong terminal to get you." She looked tired and frustrated. I felt embarrassed at being the cause. Suzanne, with typical American generosity, had offered to put me up until the retreat. With great willingness I offered to do whatever I could in exchange, pleased at the opportunity it gave me to get to know her better.

In 1992 this amazing woman, together with a few friends, started Creative Health Network. Her dream was to build a global network of people who cared about the planet and who wanted to make a difference. Her belief was that we do make a difference, that there is a divine plan, that it is we as individuals who must see that this plan unfolds upon Earth.

Amazingly dynamic, this small dark-haired woman networks tirelessly using all the tools available to her. Genuinely interested in people and admiring of their talents, Suzanne has that rare gift of seeing the best in everyone. I have seen people bloom in her presence, suddenly aware of the gifts they have to offer, gaining confidence and courage to speak out or act.

Organization though was not her strong point I discovered, as she waved a hand airily at her 'office'. Piles of papers filled every possible surface, and as I looked several papers slipped to the floor as she jolted the table in passing. Together we resumed the search for a missing item that she had abandoned in order to fetch me. Four mugs of tea later, the piles looked more ordered but we had not found the item. What I discovered instead was evidence of the vast network of friends from round the world which Suzanne has gathered to herself. There were piles of letters, many accompanied by little keepsakes or photos of smiling people standing beside her, their arm draped across her shoulders. A much loved woman, her warm spirit, great integrity and inspiring vision has touched and changed the lives of many. But one thing about this indomitable person strikes me above all else. It is her level of trust, her steadfast faith that goodness and peace will prevail on Earth.

****

"Fill us with Your creativity so that we may be empowered to bear the fruit of Your mission. Let each of our actions bear fruit in accordance with Your desire."

The Lord's Prayer translated directly from Aramaic into English

The five-day retreat was held at Mount Alverno Conference Centre, less than an hour's drive from Suzanne's home in Palo Alto. The centre was situated on the slopes of the hills above Redwood City, with a wonderful view across San Francisco Bay. Surrounding the buildings were beautifully tended grounds where lawns sloped away to wooded areas. Undisturbed by sounds of traffic, the place was a haven of tranquillity.

By the time we got there, our vehicle overflowing with the paraphernalia needed for this sort of event, people had already begun to arrive. Delight rippled around as friends were reunited; some, like me, meeting people again for the first time since the '98 conference. I was struck by how easy it is to resume friendships when there is a common bond. By the end they were more than friends. I felt I was among family.

Small groups suit my personality and to start with there were just seventeen people. It was wonderful. Sitting in a large circle, every person had the opportunity to join in discussion. There was space and time to listen and be heard for everyone. At the outset there were times when it became noisy, almost chaotic, when disagreements and ruffled feelings caused tempers to rise. The electric atmosphere crackled with discord and some looked on with dismay, wondering how the process of peace could be served by a group who exhibited so much discord amongst themselves. Yet through the psychodynamic process of voicing feelings and airing differences, we gained deeper respect and understanding for each other. It enabled us to develop a group relationship where we could work together powerfully and in harmony. By the end of day two, discord had been replaced by agreement. We had bonded as a company.

This was my first taste of conflict resolution and it was a valuable opportunity to become skilled at hearing perspectives of others, understanding the equal validity of totally opposite viewpoints.

The manageable size of the gathering meant we could all be involved in deciding the most valuable use of the time we had. The experience of peers co-creating as equals was intensely dynamic and I believe greater things were achieved in those five days than at the much larger summits where presentations and workshops are distractions to the main purpose of gathering.

As a group we chose to look at the 'process' of manifestation. For several hours we explored the 'mechanics' of how to create a container of possibility or, in other words, how to create the right conditions for something to happen rather than trying to create a specific outcome. Inevitably we came to the question, how do we move the idea of peace from the realm of thought into physical reality? I hesitated, then put forward the concept of "earth-ing through gratitude and its importance as part of the manifestation process." It was a challenging moment for me. It was the first time for my silent, silver voice to be put to the test.

By co-incidence, another member had brought audiotapes of an American, who at that time I had never heard of, named Gregg Braden. He talked about "The Lost Mode of Prayer", the prayer form of indigenous people. He was saying almost exactly the same thing. It gave me courage to suggest we try it for ourselves. Although working in agreement, all the discussions had the disadvantage of keeping us in our heads, conscious of our individuality - in harmony, yet still separate, our heads and hearts disconnected. The simple process of going outside and connecting with Earth in a state of gratitude changed that.

It took two attempts before what I was trying to communicate was understood. On the first occasion, I watched frustrated as some people strolled along concrete paths, not attempting to walk on the grass.

Others, standing statue-still upon the grass, tilted their faces towards the sun in rapt communion with the Divine Presence. Returning inside, it was possible to discern a change but I could feel that they 'hadn't got it'. I was insistent that we discussed experiences and the internal process in which individuals had been involved. Quickly it emerged that recognition and gratitude had been directed by most outwards and upwards to the Source of Creation. This was not what I meant, I explained. We need to direct our attention and gratitude downwards towards Earth herself for this purpose.

Out we trooped again allowing time and space for self-consciousness to evaporate for I was suggesting something some of them had never done before. Spreading out around the grounds people sought communion with Earth finding their own private expression. Some hugged trees or rocks but many just lay upon the grass. Everyone now had their attention on the Earth. Forty minutes later, I began calling people back. It took a long time for people to return. The experience for most had been very profound. Sitting again in the circle, we kept our silence, unwilling to break into the experience of 'a peace that goes beyond all understanding'. We were out of our heads and into our hearts, where deepest wisdom and understanding resides. Peace had manifested in physical reality. Through the attempt to establish right relationship with Earth we had become a balanced and potent group consciousness. We had truly become One.

On the final day, we agreed that our insights should be applied at the forthcoming Australian Healing Summit 2000. Many of us were thinking of the need for healing the racialist mentality still harboured by many. We believed we now had the metaphysical understanding needed to effect greater and more rapid change in the areas of racial and ideological discord.

****

On the way back to Palo Alto, talk about what had taken place on the five days naturally threaded its way in and out of the conversation. Talking about the "Earth-ing" experience, Suzanne unwittingly validated the impression I got in Spain. She volunteered, "I asked Earth what she wanted from me. The word I got was 'Recognition'."

CHAPTER TEN

"The ancient calendars, almost universally, point to this time
as being unique not only in terms of human history but to
earth history, to geological history as well....
"We are being asked to remember, to know the mystery
within, collectively, as we approach this time in history which
the Ancients call the Shift of the Ages."
Gregg Braden. Video presentation "Awakening to Zero Point"

I arrived back in England at the end of October, two months away from the New Millennium. An atmosphere of expectancy hung in the air; the sense of imminent change almost palpable. People seemed to be gripped by a fever for getting rid of everything superfluous to their future lives. It took various forms: unseasonal spring-cleans, walking out of marriages or jobs, major changes of lifestyle. It seemed people wanted to be freer, lighter, unhampered. I could feel the same instinctive urgency within myself.

The moment came. We moved into 2000, the passage marked by all those unforgettable celebrations across the globe. For twenty-four hours we celebrated as the Family of Man, able to follow the passing of the old and the dawning of the new, the sun rising for each country in turn as pictures were beamed into our homes by satellite. The whole world united in a giant party.

The early days of the new millennium were marked for me by a paradox that surfaced and began to dominate my life. It gave me the opportunity to look afresh at how two complete opposites can be true simultaneously.

I became very aware of the choice between which aspect of the paradox - the positive or the negative - I made my reality. It was a question of focus. Did I see the glass as half full or half empty? Looking at the glass half full filled me with encouragement and optimism, while the reality of half-empty created fear of lack and depression.

But it did not end there. The experience of paradox continued to develop. In my peace and contentment with aloneness, I felt it was a supportive Universe, and yet I felt isolated, lonely and unsupported as I struggled all by myself with 'flu. The same was true in my experience around financial abundance. I felt affluent yet couldn't buy simple things that I needed. Two realities. I was experiencing the multifaceted nature of Truth spoken of by the crystal voice.

Internally, I shifted to a middle position able to experience both truths simultaneously. I became comfortable with embracing the paradox. I felt like a parent who is able to love and accept two children of totally opposite natures. But nothing stays constant. The insight was not yet fully integrated and I lost the experience. The pressure of finding more than two and half thousand pounds for Australia tipped the scales and gradually my reality and experience slid into one of lack. I began to lose that sense of trust that steered my life.

For the first time I began to doubt the possibility of going. Constantly aware of scarcity now, I became increasingly anxious about the huge sums of money needed for the trip.

It was at this moment, when I was on the point of

withdrawing, that the axe appeared in my life; the axe with two faces, one pale, the other dark and shiny, light and dark coming together along a cutting edge. Whatever else it symbolized for us on that cold March day, on the personal level I had been given something that perfectly symbolized embracing the paradox. It revived my sense of trust.

If I put out the intention, I thought, the money would be found.

I looked at ways to raise the money. Amongst other things I started The Celebration Dinner Network. It was a scheme that provided self-employed people who had humanitarian interests with a chance to network for themselves while celebrating the good things in life over a "special deal" meal in one of the best restaurants in Bath. The membership fees went towards my air-ticket. But there was still a huge shortfall.

I started to search for sponsors. I contacted 'The Bath Chronicle' as a starting point. They were intrigued by the story and willing to print a short article accompanied by photographs on their 'collectors' page. The photographer duly came and took pictures of me from every angle, holding the axe. Although disappointed that the story was not going to be printed in a well-read section of the paper, I was grateful for their willingness to help.

All my efforts exhausted me and I succumbed to an attack of influenza, which laid me out for days.

In bed, there was plenty of time to think. I relived finding the axe and recalled my thoughts. Bushmen in Africa.

'Bush' man in Australia. Was there an association between them?

At this point another significant synchronicity took place. I had nothing to do but watch a great deal of television and as a result I happened to see something I might otherwise have missed - a TV documentary called 'Ape Man'. Throughout the film were shots of the Cape Coast beaches of South Africa and of modern day Bushmen squatting round their fire, the vast star bowl of the southern hemisphere night sky twinkling overhead. The documentary spoke of evidence that pointed to the probability that ancestors of the Bushman migrated over time into Europe and eastwards, across the tectonic plates before they split, to populate Asia and finally Australia. I thought of those ancient people trekking vast distances across the globe, successive generations pushing further and further east over thousands of years. Emerging from my sickbed, I was delighted to find that a good - if conservative - account of the axe story had been printed in 'The Bath Chronicle' earlier in the week. A large photograph of Bushmen, announcing the forthcoming documentary on the preceding page, further gripped my attention.

CHAPTER ELEVEN

"I believe in the Tinkerbell Theory. If enough people believe in it, it will happen."
Tim Smit. Chief Executive of the Eden Project

In the months following the discovery of the axe, I thought deeply about how we could apply what we had done at Mount Alverno to healing the Aboriginal Wound, indeed, healing the wound of indigenous people everywhere. The conviction grew that one route was through demonstrating recognition and gratitude to Earth Mother and Her caretakers simultaneously. I could imagine that for the Aborigines, who are so inextricably linked with Mother Earth, any acts of gratitude and recognition of Her could prove to be an important step in their own healing, particularly if this was coupled with the acknowledgment that amongst them are caretakers of an ancient wisdom containing knowledge which can demonstrate for us how to live in harmony with Earth. We need to become surfers on this great wave of change instead of being victims tumbled helplessly in the breakers.

As if to mirror my thoughts, I began to see evidence popping up in articles and in television documentaries to show that others too are beginning to perceive this need. I became aware of an increasing flood of Native Americans, from North and South, circulating the globe, sharing the spiritual teachings of their people. It was evidence of a growing understanding that it is time for people around the planet to share knowledge with each other and for the spiritual wisdom of the Western

World to be drawn together with the wisdom and knowledge held by tribal elders.

I knew that this was an idea whose time had come and nothing could stop it gaining momentum. An awakening is gradually taking place both in modern society and amongst indigenous people - an awakening that is potentially paving the way to forgiveness.

All this was in my mind as I made arrangements to go with a group of fellow healers and peace workers to Uluru (Ayer's Rock) following the summit. Ahead of time, I naively attempted to fix up meetings with Aboriginal elders. I scoured websites for email addresses that were likely to lead me to the right people and made costly phone calls to Australia. The spirit of evangelism ran high. I saw this as an opportunity for white people from different parts of the world to learn, first hand, from Aboriginal mouths how to be in a good relationship with the Earth - an opportunity to learn how to bring ourselves into alignment with Her as we all go through this great shift.

My hopes were dashed. I was told firmly this was not something that could easily be arranged in the time that was available. The Anangu, Aboriginal landowners of Kata Tjuta National Park at Uluru, were a law unto themselves. The best I could do was to send a letter of my wishes to the Kata Tjuta Cultural Centre and hope for the best.

Disappointed, I decided the best course of action then was to 'tune in and tune up' and put out a call on the 'higher planes' announcing my intent. After all, I reasoned to myself, it is now well documented that the Aboriginal people have extraordinary powers of telepathy. Feeling the appropriateness of my actions, I cleared my sitting room of clutter and created a little medicine wheel on the floor. Stones I had collected and kept from Severn beach formed the ring. Within it I placed the axe with the stone finger upon it, and natural objects that I had accumulated - stones, feathers, shells. At the heart of the circle was the candle lit by the Peace Flame. With quiet ceremony, I settled myself facing the wheel and lit the candle. I remembered, as I did so, the remarkable act of bringing peace flames from many countries together as one flame, and how members of the Australian air force kept the Australian Peace Flame, brought over on a military plane, alight throughout the journey.

Clearing my mind of the day's pre-occupations, I sent a prayer out to the angelic realms for protection and then turned my focus towards Australia. I used imagination to help me in visualizing a golden cord linking me to the great red centre at the heart of the subcontinent. Silently I sent out the mental message that I was coming; that I was committed to interracial reconciliation. I was the keeper of a stone axe that held the memory of ancient knowledge and which was being used for healing the rift between the black and white races.

Would the ones with whom I should work make themselves known? Please!

****

When I found the axe my thought had been that it should be left in Australia with Aboriginal people. This plan was revised in May following an encounter in a 'grandmother circle'.

I had taken a group away to the Land's End Peninsula in Cornwall. I chose the place for its beauty and for the sense of uncompromising integrity in the landscape. I also chose it because I love it. For years it has been my Mecca when I have felt in need of renewal.

The weather was appalling as we set out and continued unpromising for much of the journey. Then optimism rose at the sight of a break in the clouds, as we travelled the final miles beyond St Ives. By the time we reached The Old Chapel Backpackers Hostel in Zennor, a watery sun was managing to bring some colour into the damp, grey landscape. A small window of finer weather seemed just possible.

In a fit of madness, I suggested climbing to the top of Zennor Hill, which loomed over the tiny hamlet. The scrambling climb up the rocky hill was difficult. Wet gorse pricked through our clothing, scratching our legs. But finally making it to the top, we were rewarded by three hundred and sixty degrees of fabulous view. Standing in a natural stone circle, we could look for miles in all directions. The sculptural forms of strange rocky outcrops stood in dark silhouette as the sun slipped over the horizon far out to sea. It was getting late and we were nervous about the climb down in failing light. However, having climbed all this way, we wanted to mark the occasion. I described the form of prayer used by indigenous people to bring rain.

Couldn't we use it to create the opposite? Together we sat in a ring, our backs against the rocks and focused on seeing the full moon sailing through a clear night sky and in the way of Native American people, gave thanks that it would be so.

Just before we began, I put the axe in the centre of the ring. It felt right.

It was for only a few minutes, but it was almost dark when we opened our eyes again. Seizing the axe I scrambled to my feet and, urging the others to hurry, started back along the narrow path.

The climb back down the hill was a nightmare. I was uncomfortably aware of my responsibility for everyone's safety, as time and again we found our way blocked by gorse and steep drops. In the dimming light these hazards became increasingly hard to see. It was a border collie, the pet of one of our number, which came to our rescue just as I was beginning to feel really anxious. "Don't worry. He'll sniff out the way back," she reassured me. Bringing the dog to heel, she stroked his head for a moment and then issued her instruction. "Find!" she cried pointing down the hill. Nose down, the dog cast about amongst the gorse, the black and white plume of his tail just visible, then picking up our earlier trail scent, he was off. In a straggling, struggling line we followed the dog as he unerringly sniffed out the route we had taken, back down to the safety of the road.

****

*"The world of reality has its limits;
the world of imagination is boundless."*
Jean-Jacques Rousseau

*"Shoot for the moon.
Even if you miss it you will land among the stars."*
Anon

We awoke next morning to blazing sunshine. The countryside danced alive into vibrant colour. Butterflies and bumblebees, making up for lost time, droned and flitted amongst the coloured jewels of nature. Jerseys came off and skin, blushing pink with pleasure in the sun, breathed thankfully once more. All through the day and into the evening the window of clear weather held fast.

As sunset approached, we gathered at the home of Celtic blacksmith and sculptor, Hamish Miller, famed for his skill in dowsing and his knowledge of earth energy lines. As a dowser and geomancer he has dedicated much of his time to bringing back harmony in areas of disturbance. We wound our way along grassy walkways through a parkland setting lovingly created and tended by Hamish's life partner Ba, where nature and cultivation have been carefully combined to create an area of great beauty. Our footsteps took us past clumps of nodding scented bluebells and the first magenta blush of foxgloves standing straight and tall, until we emerged into a clearing on the side of a hill. Its backdrop view stretched for miles across rolling arable land to the distant ridge above Nancledra. Into the turf had been cut a 'Seed of Life' mandala, and it was round this we gathered to perform a brief ceremony. An atmosphere of peace descended over the landscape as the shadows lengthened and a rabbit, undisturbed by our presence, emerged from the gorse to feed. In a brief ceremony we focused on our relationship with Earth. The Taurus full moon, its association strong with Earth and Nature, was nowhere to be seen; yet in the meditative state we were in, we felt the strength of its energy. As dark descended we trooped inside. More was in store for us. A traditional ceremony of Native American origin had been organized by a one of the group. Called a 'grandmothers' circle', it provided us with an opportunity to visit one of eight 'grandmothers' for insight. We sat in a circle by the compass point relating to the 'grandmother' we wished to 'visit'. Predictably, I chose Grandmother Earth.

I closed my eyes and listened to the soft beat of the grandmother drum, letting its sound carry me far away into another space. With a jolt I felt I had arrived somewhere. My internal eyes opened. I was back in the roundhouse on the Esselen sacred grounds. This time I was alone in the deep silence, looking at the dust-filled shaft of sunlight pouring through the smoke hole in the centre, smelling the faint acrid smell of past fires.

"Grandmother, can you tell me what to do with the axe head?" I asked.

Suddenly I saw my two hands holding the axe head going from place to place - many places. I understood then that my axe would be instrumental in connecting me with a group of Aboriginal people who would bring me insight and wisdom, but that it was not to stay there. For the first time I realized that the axe was to be used to connect me to people from many lands, not just Aborigines. This was a surprising and unexpected revelation but as it turned out, it was exactly what happened.

Following that, I was shown many wonderful and perplexing things before I heard the sound of the grandmother drum calling me back. I had not seen the grandmother, I realized. "Grandmother, what do you look like?" I asked.

"Surely you know that. Here you are surrounded by me - within me. I am above you, below you and around you. I am everywhere you look." With that I saw I was back in the roundhouse with dust trickling through the roof spaces. I suddenly felt how womb-like it was.

"Grandmother have you a gift for our group? Please!" I cried.

A giant hand appeared holding a giant pearl, its satin sheen gleaming with a soft creamy silken light.

"This, the pearl of wisdom, I give the group as my gift." The giant hand was raised aloft to the sky holding the pearl in its palm. Then the hand withdrew leaving the pearl hanging there and I saw it was the full moon shining its soft light down upon us. I understood then that Earth Mother had indeed heard and responded to our prayer the night before on Zennor Hill. Her gift was the corridor of clear and clement weather.

The drum tapping softly, called me back into the room. I closed my internal eyes and opened my physical ones. The three-D world, solidly matter of fact, surrounded me. But there, hanging in the sky, like a bit of left-over magic, was the round golden moon, its soft light pouring in through the window.

As we drove back into The Old Chapel car park at midnight, the clouds were once again scudding across the face of the moon. Next morning the leaden skies had returned, the perfect day and beautiful moonrise of the day before just a wonderful memory.

Before I left Zennor I made a discovery. I found out that this part of Cornwall was the centre of much Neolithic activity. A short distance down the road were quarries where greenstone, a highly prized type of granite, was mined for making ceremonial axes. Unknown to me until this moment, Zennor Hill, my favourite place for several years, sheltered from sight Zennor Quoit, one of the largest Neolithic burial chambers of the area.

****

In one of my long phone calls to Carlo Hawkwalker on my return home from Cornwall, we discussed the need for me to find the source of my axe.

"When your axe is taken home, memories and wisdom that is locked within its crystal structure will be released. It is then that you will truly know the knowledge it contains."

I knew this was true but was reluctant to let geologists cut a fragment from its perfect form. In the meantime, plans for a quest down-under were gaining momentum. I was off to find a group of people and the axe was going to lead me to them.

CHAPTER TWELVE

"We are all droplets in the Ocean of God."
Sir George Trevelyan

On August the 3rd, six days before I left, I had a vision of the place where my axe had to go. I sat in my sitting room with the axe in my hands. The polished surface reflected a soft sheen. Just as months before on the Severn Beach, I could make out the wise old face of a bearded man sitting with eyes closed in meditative repose. I followed his example and closed my eyes. I asked the same question that I had asked many times before without getting an answer.

"Where does my axe need to go?"

Suddenly I got a series of vivid images.

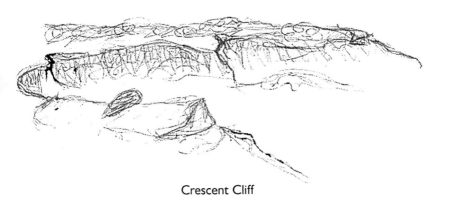

Crescent Cliff

I was shown the flat top of high land. It was an area with cliffs that curved in a crescent moon shape. Sitting on top of a flat rock was my axe looking as if it was surveying the scene. I could look down over a tree-covered landscape from there. The image switched to heavily leaning eucalypts with white bark. I had an impression of stepping down a bank and walking across a dried riverbed. The impressions were so strong and images so clear, I reached for my notebook and drew a sketch of what I had seen. Tucking it away at the bottom of my suitcase, I forgot about this until weeks later, I stood on the rock where, in my mental picture, the axe had been and again saw the scene, this time with my physical eyes.

****

I arrived in Queensland less exhausted than I expected to be. Stepping off the plane at Proserpine, I was struck immediately by how like South Africa, the home of my birth, it was. Tall eucalyptus trees and dry brown grass surrounded the airstrip. Snuffing the air as I walked across the tarmac to the tiny terminal building, even the smells seemed familiar. The carefully tended plants bordering the path were ones I knew from childhood days. I felt at home.

In the breezy warmth, waiting for my suitcase, I grinned at familiar faces. The journey from Sydney had passed in a jet-lagged haze of pleasure with delegates I knew. I had spotted the first of many familiar faces in the departure lounge as I queued, my ticket and passport in hand. Suddenly the feeling of being small and vulnerable vanished. I was no longer alone.

Nicola, who had led the sound workshop in Monterey, grinned back. A sense of sisterhood flowed between us. Together we stood and watched the tractor, like a lopsided insect, crawl across the airfield dragging a precariously leaning mountain of luggage behind it. A brawny Queenslander jumped down from the tractor and with effortless ease swung one suitcase after another to the ground at a quicker rate than we could retrieve them. He made some wisecrack, which we, our ears not yet adjusted to Australian voices, did not understand. We responded with gales of laughter nonetheless. With the knowledge that our gruelling journey was almost at an end, our spirits were high for the short journey to Shute Harbour, where a waiting boat edged skittishly away from the jetty, tugging at its moorings like a nervous horse.

The ferryboat headed out into the Whitsunday Passage and threaded its way between a cluster of Whitsunday islands towards our destination. The water swelled around the bow as it sliced a pathway. It boiled past the sides and slipped away in a trailing stream of milky greenness. Spray splashed my face and I licked my lips, savouring the salt.

Sea - the mightiest of all the realms on Earth. How amazing, I thought, that one day this same water would splash against the shores of Britain.

Rounding a small islet, we got our first glimpse of South Molle Island. It rose out of the water, an unspoilt tropical paradise, its hilly contours covered with lush forest and yellow beaches rimming the waterline.

As we drew nearer, we could make out a long jetty and the small group of figures waiting to greet us. Soon we could make out individual palm trees, coconuts hanging green and pendulous over the sand, and, discretely hidden from sight behind the trees, a cluster of buildings, our home for the duration of the conference.

Looking down into the water as I stepped onto the jetty, I was taken aback by the sight of several huge fish churning the water surface. They were beautifully marked with dark stripes along their flat sides. One fish broke surface mouthing the air with faint popping sounds before it sank again, a petulant flick of its grey tail sending it knifing away through the water like an underwater sail. "What are they?" I cried.

"Bat fish," the man helping me ashore replied. "Very common here. You'll see plenty of those!"

My room looked out to sea towards the Whitsunday passage and the Great Barrier Reef. I stood on the balcony drinking it all in. Out there were whales and dolphins. I pictured them swimming back and forth along ancient migration trails that went back to the beginning of time.

Above my head multicoloured parrots, their jewelled plumage of red, blue and green fluffed up in rage, squabbled in screeching argument in the palm tree overshadowing my balcony. Litter louts of the bird-world, they dropped a steady rain of discarded bits as they fed. I watched their brightly coloured progress from tree to tree until they were out of sight, then went down to the beach.

The water line was edged with coral fragments, evidence of the damage happening to the reef further out. Holding a finger of coral, I studied its form, a tiny exquisite piece of nature, sides covered in spiralling bobbles against a bed of filigree. I wondered what colour had once stained its pure white surface.

More than forty years had passed since I last stood ankle deep in tropical waters peering into coral pools. I recalled the magic and wonder of standing at low tide on the reefs fringing Inhaca Island off the coast of Mozambique, gazing at the exotic and brilliantly coloured underwater garden.

For a long time I was motionless, gazing out to sea as the sun dipped over the hills in late afternoon. I stood ankle deep, surrounded by the dancing sparkle of sunlight on water, and felt all the negativity stored within me drain away through the soles of my feet to be lost forever in the vastness of the ocean. Totally at peace, I idly contemplated a drop of water hanging from my fingertip. Contained within its form were all the elements of 'oceanness'. It dripped back into the sea and merging, was lost. Yet I had knowledge that that single individual drop existed. How like that drop I was in the infinite ocean of existence, I mused.

Leaving the sea, I climbed upwards through the forest along a winding track. Following the sounds of rustling, I spotted a pair of black wildfowl scratching through the leafy forest floor as they made leisurely progress deeper into the bush.

My eye was caught by the black and white flicker of flight.

A kookaburra landed on a branch close by and cocked his head to watch me inquisitively. Remembering the childhood round I used to sing, I sang to him and watched him turn his head this way and that. But he remained silent. It became a contest of who would move first. As evening was approaching I gave way first and wandered on. Behind me the Kookaburra finally gave his verdict on my performance. His rolling laugh followed me through the trees and I could hear him laughing still when I emerged into a clearing surrounding a hanging rock. I sat for a while like a queen gazing out over my dominion. In the silence broken only by the sound of the strong breeze buffeting against the giant rock looming protectively over me, I was acutely aware of my surroundings. The smell of dry earth mingled with the pungency of hot vegetation. The rock beneath me felt vibrant and alive, contradicting the view so often held that Earth is an inanimate object.

Below me was dense forest going down to the sea. Beyond the forest, the spine of the island undulated away into the distance under a covering of bush and long grass. A flight of white cockatoos skimmed over the tree canopy and, landing in a noisy swoop, disappeared from sight. High overhead I caught sight of the dark, wheeling form of a solitary eagle.

The breeze was freshening. A sea of wild grasses on the distant slopes rippled with silken light, catching alight in the orange fire of the setting sun. Turning, I hurried back to the hotel, my homeward steps speeding now to beat the darkness that was racing in to flood the valleys.

CHAPTER THIRTEEN

"Clasp the hands and know the thoughts
of men in other lands...."
John Masefield

"Our deepest fear is not that we are inadequate.
Our deepest fear is that we are powerful beyond measure.
It is our light, not our darkness, that most frightens us
We ask ourselves, who am I to be brilliant, gorgeous,
talented and fabulous? Actually who are you not to be?
You are a child of God.
Your playing small doesn't serve the world.
There's nothing enlightened about shrinking so that
other people won't feel insecure around you..
We were born to make manifest
the Glory of God that is within us.
It's not just in some of us; it's in everyone.
And as we let our own light shine,
we unconsciously give other people permission
to do the same.
As we are liberated from our own fear,
our presence automatically liberates other."
1994 Inaugural Speech, Nelson Mandela

The conference turned out to be much smaller in size than I had expected. There were fewer than a hundred people present. But a small gathering can be more powerful and I had high hopes. At this week long conference, inspiring projects would be publicised. There would be news of people making a difference. Personal success stories would be shared; concrete examples of the changes taking place; the movements of change spreading upwards from grass roots level, quietly replacing old and destructive paradigms with new models for living in harmony.

Amongst the delegates was N'Dhala, a beautiful part-Aboriginal woman from Central Australia. A shy person, she maintained a low profile throughout. I showed her my axe and together we talked about how I might connect with the Aborigines around Uluru. I spoke of the visions and guidance. She listened with interest but made no comment. There was nothing she could think of that might be of help.

It was N'Dhala who quietly helped us to understand many things, patiently explaining differences in custom. The Aboriginal race is a deeply feeling people, she explained. They connect heart to heart. Much of what we do is unnecessary in their view. Because we have lost much of our sensitivity, we have to demonstrate more so as to share or feel an experience. Rather than embracing, Aborigines make gentle hand contact. The touch, light and brief, is meaningful and can convey far more than the hug. When we did not understand why she broke ranks in the greetings dance, she explained that she had to break the eye contact. In Aboriginal way it is offensive to make deep eye contact, especially when you first meet people. The western practice of gazing into another's eyes for deeper connection is unnecessary in their culture for they know they are always in contact on soul level. As with touch, eye contact is fleeting and shy and full of meaning.

For the first three days of the conference, we were privileged to have members of the Birri Nation, the tribal custodians of the Whitsunday Islands, amongst us. 'Auntie' was an elder whose quiet and gentle manner did not disguise her air of authority. When she spoke we listened. We learned much through her about recognition of and respect for each other. Not all of the insights were comfortable. In our first meeting we listened as Auntie and her nephew Keith told us what they wished us to hear. They spoke of violence, of the massacres, of their land being stolen. They talked sadly of how their history and culture is being lost. The few remaining who still know the Law are elderly. They spoke of the lost generation of mixed race children who were forcibly taken from their families to be raised in the cities, in orphanages or the homes of 'good white families'. They spoke of their sense of betrayal, of hurt and outrage that the Australian government still won't officially apologize to Aboriginal people.

Then someone asked a question about the personal effects of prejudice. There was silence while Auntie looked at us measuring our responsiveness and willingness to hear what she had to say. The account of racial hatred and indifference was painful to hear. For me, having been brought up in South Africa by parents involved in race relations, the story though shocking was absolutely believable. But I could see by the expression on the face of the woman seated beside me that she thought the account was biased and an exaggeration.

Her attitude was changed by the interruption of a beautiful, dark-haired, young woman whose skin had the olive tones of Latin people. In a short and moving account she verified everything already described. As a child she had been mistaken for being part Aboriginal, a target of prejudice because of her dark skin. Adults and children alike tormented her. Teachers would never give her top grades even when her exam papers showed a hundred per cent. A highly intelligent child, she went through school in the lowest stream. denied all privileges like the Aboriginal pupils. But it was in the playground that she suffered most. Being pretty added to her disadvantage. She was the target of jealousy as well as hate. At one point her tormentors formed a lynch party on the playground and she nearly lost her life. She was close to unconsciousness before an adult intervened. The culprits were given no more than a reprimand, but the rope marks on her neck were still there as a constant reminder and it was clear she was emotionally scarred by the experience. As she verified the sense of hurt and outrage, suffering and lack of self-esteem, the trauma of her childhood years was evident. There was deep empathy on the faces of the Aboriginal people but I thought I could detect a sense of relief that their story was being corroborated by another. I felt sadness that there were any amongst us who needed a white person's corroboration before they would believe; a small insidious sign of prejudice lingering in the unconscious mind to trip up even the best intentioned.

One by one, others who had been marked by prejudice began to share their stories. It was an extraordinary afternoon where black and white met and merged on the common ground of pain, suffering and injustice while others held them in a space of safety. Tears trickled down faces, dripping unheeded off chins as understanding and fellowship flowed between black and white delegates. As the afternoon drew to a close there was a sense of catharsis, for some real healing and forgiveness had been set in motion.

We gained a lot from our contact with each other and some intense friendships were forged. Bea Agins' work with the Achual Indians of the Peruvian Amazon fascinated all of the Aboriginal delegates particularly Keith, Maurice and Terence, who were members of a dance and drama troupe. They were able to relate to many of the Indian practices and creation stories. A mutual empathy developed between Bea and the three Aboriginal men. Late one evening they sat by the side of the pool talking together around a table. Leaning on their elbows, heads close together, they shared, compared and laughed together. I was in another group, deep in conversation, when suddenly I heard the incongruous sound of Peruvian Pan Pipes playing a pop version of Beethoven's Ninth Symphony. I looked round. Bea was dancing with Terence. They whirled round each other weaving back and forth between other dancers. I looked on amazed at the extraordinarily incongruous sight of Terence dancing his Aboriginal dances to Peruvian panpipe music. I watched as he glided like an eagle, moved with the sinuousness of a snake, became a grooming kangaroo. He danced alive the Ancestral Beings as he told the creation stories through his movements. I reached for the camera. I took five flash photographs. They were the only photographs taken at the Summit that did not come out as expected. Instead of a dancing figure, all I got were beautiful swirling lines of light.

Some said that the pictures I took showed the energy of his dance. Perhaps they did.

CHAPTER FOURTEEN

"Much of my life today is filled with anger.
It is as if something vital has been torn out of me.
The vessel that I am has been broken and fragmented into
little pieces that don't fit together anymore."
'Song of the Circle' Barry Brailsford

The Summit was both intensely frustrating and wonderful. Frustrating because there were communication difficulties between delegates and organizers - we failed to implement many of the insights gained at the 'think-tank retreat' in California in 1999. Wonderful because we heard about inspiring new peace ventures and were able to be with Aboriginal delegates sharing visions we have in common. There were moments of uncomfortable insight highlighted by the misunderstandings and difficulties that can arise when observing cross-cultural courtesies. It was a learning curve for all.

I was particularly drawn to N'Dhala and deeply appreciative of the times we spent alone talking about spiritual philosophy and sharing insights. Immersed in our mutual interests as we were, our conversations failed to touch on personal details and this lack of information sprang several surprises for me later on.

At last the moment arrived for which I had been waiting. The Summit ended and I was led unerringly to the place and people with whom I needed to connect. But as had happened before with my visions, none of my assumptions about the details were correct. Once again real life proved to be more interesting than my imaginings.

A number of us, imbued with the high energy of the gathering, headed for Uluru under the leadership of Heather Sixt. Passionate about Aboriginal culture, this small woman has committed herself to running tours geared to putting people in touch with the special energy and relationship that Aboriginal people in the Northern Territory have with their ancestral lands. The trip she organized for us would, she promised, give us opportunities to be with Aboriginal people from the Northern Territories.

Frustrated over what I saw as missed opportunities at the Summit, I found it significant that the journey to Uluru was fraught with difficulties. At Proserpine airport it was discovered that the tickets held by the three organizers amongst us were invalid. We looked at each other numb with dismay. Plane connections had been missed on the way to the Summit and the re-routing of their flights then was the cause of this current problem. I viewed it as the Universe mirroring back to them that in forgetting what we had previously learned, there had been missed connections and lost opportunities at the conference. In my frustration I had lost my understanding that there is a Greater Plan at work and that my small will did not stand a chance against the Will of the Numinous One.

There was nothing for it but for the rest of us to go on ahead and hope that they would be able to catch up with us. As we walked across the tarmac to the small plane we turned and waved farewell at the faces we could see pressed forlornly against the window.

Fortunately our trip to Uluru was via Sydney, where we

stopped for a night, thus providing them with the chance to catch up. Tired and dishevelled, they arrived just as we sat down for dinner and the evening passed swiftly as, garrulous with relief, they regaled us with their adventures.

Early the following morning I had a brief and totally unexpected encounter with N'Dhala. With plenty of time on my hands, I was strolling through the terminal building when I literally bumped into her. I was astonished.

"What are you doing here?" I asked.

"I am on my way to board my connection for Alice," she said. She was hurrying.

Touching me on the shoulder as she turned to go, she added, "See you in a couple of days!"

"What do you mean?" I called after her.

Walking backwards she shouted her reply, "I am organizing an experience for you with my mob on my homeland. Bye!"

She turned and disappeared into the crowd. Suddenly things I had heard mentioned began to fall into place. N'Dhala, I remembered being told, lived in Central Australia in the Northern Territories. I was delighted at the thought that I was going to see more of her. She had so much to share.

Later, she told me how she found her way back to Unity,

guided in the same way that I was by 'a lot of help from the other side'. Like me, she had followed the open doors of synchronicity, which took her back home. "I even saw my homeland clearly in my mind's eye before I set foot in the place." she said.

As I watched her walk out of sight, there was no way of knowing how important she would become to me in the near future. Yet I felt this brief, chance meeting was significant and wondered about it all the way to Uluru.

On board the plane, I thought about some of the things I had heard at the conference. I wondered if it was true that there had been an unofficial policy until quite recently of 'dilute and disperse', where Aboriginal women were raped and the resulting children removed with deliberate intent to dilute Aboriginal blood as a way of breaking their ties with the land. I remembered what Auntie and Keith had said about a 'lost generation' of mixed race children. The thought horrified me.

That there was some truth in it seemed to be born out in the story I heard of an Aboriginal man who fathered more than twenty children in an unconscious attempt to re-create the tribe that had been lost to him in childhood.

So many fractured lives, so many damaged people in the world needing to understand the origin of their emotional and psychological wounds.

CHAPTER FIFTEEN

*"Greet the mountain standing tall, the ancestor that
holds the spirit of those who gave their bones to the heights.
Honour their memory and keep the sacred secure
within the stone."*
'Song of the Circle' Barry Brailsford

*"There is only natural knowing, and no matter how you
come by it, it is the same in the end. You get a glimpse of
the imagination of nature. You become gloriously entangled
in the web of the universe. This is our right in Earth's estate.
It is our inheritance."*
Lyall Watson - Gifts of Unknown Things

No film seen could prepare me for the experience of
going to Uluru. The fiery red soil of the region hit me like
a challenge. Although desert, the land was vibrantly alive.
It pulsated with energy and I was acutely conscious that
it is governed by a different Law - the Law of Tjukurpa.
It is a Law that does not recognize anything outside of
the natural creation and natural order of things. It
provides the rules for behaviour and living together, how
to care for one another and the land that supports
everything. It is the land of dreamtime magic. I was
conscious that I needed to walk with respect for this was
a place where ancient gods of creation roam.

Soaring above the surrounding landscape, Uluru and Kata
Tjuta awed us by their living presence as we approached.
These vast out-thrusts of rock sat upon the land like giant
creatures with scaly chameleon skins of constantly
changing fiery colour. We watched Uluru's rich gold

against the backdrop of vivid blue sky, giving way to burnished orange, intense crimson and finally, purple-black surrounded by an aura of magenta and violet, as the sun slipped below the horizon. Even the fact that this was a far from solitary experience, with coach loads of other tourists sharing the event, could not detract from the awesomeness of the occasion.

The fact that there were so many people around and that we were constantly moving from one site to another bothered me intensely. How was it going to be possible for the axe and me to connect with the right people and place? As our time at Uluru was gradually used up with no sign of slowing the hectic schedule, I began to feel a sense of desperation. I had to find time and space alone at "the rock" in order to tune in and find out what to do next.

My chance came on the 21st of August. Although we had been asked by the Aboriginal custodians not to climb the rock that is sacred to them, three of the group decided they had to do it. When the coach dropped them off, I seized the opportunity to be dropped off too, and spent three precious hours alone wandering around the base.

The calls of climbers, crawling like a rope of ants up and down the treacherous rocky surface, quickly receded as I moved away through the bush and soon I was surrounded by the deep sleepy silence of mid-day. Only the rustling sounds of small creatures and insects could be heard as they scurried and crawled out of sight in the clumps of spinifex grass. The pungent smell of aromatic bushes and hot rock filled the air as I skirted the base of Uluru. I looked up the sheer rock at the cracks and stains upon the surface, remembering how each represented something in Aboriginal mythology. I gazed into the upside down world of deep silent pools that reflected the rocky walls and sky overhead with impossible clarity.

Dreaming Pools.

Dreaming still, I wandered. I felt out of time in another dimension.

As I roamed I was conscious of Tjukurpa, The Law, in operation. It was all around me.

It was in the landscape itself. I was aware of the relationship between everything; everything finely balanced in interdependent existence.

Looking up at the soaring rock face of Uluru, I recalled that every feature upon its surface tells part of the creation stories; physical testament to the feats performed during the creation period by beings whose direct descendants are the people of the area, the Anangu. For them, the landscape features that I was gazing at in awe are the embodiment of their spirit ancestors, evidence that these beings still exist.

I stepped off the Mala trail to pick a wild fig. The fruit was recognizable as a fig but it was very small and, though sweet, had little of the succulent flesh of the European variety. As I nibbled the fruit, I gazed around noting the flowers. They did not grow in clusters like wild flowers in England. In this land of space the plants grew apart so that the first impression was of sparseness. Gradually I realized that this impression was wrong. Flowers were everywhere, many of them daisy-like. Others I recognized as everlasting flowers. By me, its straggling stems supported by spinifex, a plant bloomed in lilac coloured profusion. The desert scrubland was alive with vivid points of colour.

I wandered further, meandering back and forth, stopping frequently to examine things that caught my attention. Finally I came to a cave I had visited with the others earlier in the day. It was an incredible formation: long, shallow and scooped into the base of The Rock like the curling arc of a frozen wave. Standing within it, looking down its length into a spiralling vortex at the end, I felt like a surfer in a wave tunnel.

I found a ledge I had perched upon during the earlier visit and sat down, closing my eyes.

Peace overtook me.

I had time now to think of the Aboriginal people I had met on South Molle Island. I thought of the pain of past injustices spoken about with quiet dignity by Auntie. I thought of her nephew Keith and his passion to share Aboriginal culture through story and dance, of Terence, the 'shape shifter', who became the animals he danced, and of quiet down-to-earth Maurice, whose clever hands had fashioned the beautiful didgeridoos which thrilled us all. In the quietness of the cave I tuned in, asking for guidance about how to find those with whom I needed to connect.

In retrospect it is hard to know whether what took place next was real or imagined. The powerful energy of Uluru can play strange tricks on the imagination but at the time I was convinced everything occurred just as I now relate it. I believed it happened in response to my plea and was profoundly affected by it. As I left the cave, my glance fell upon a large boulder beside the path, shaped like a horseshoe. I had been told earlier that the Aboriginal symbol for a sitting person is a U-shape. As I registered this, I heard, once again, the silent, silver voice that I had heard many months before on Severn Beach.

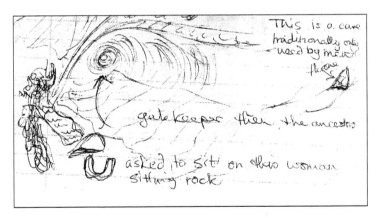

"Become a sitting person," it said.

I sat, positioning my bottom and legs on the rocky surface. Seated in this way I looked directly into the spiralling vortex of rock at the cave's end.

"What now?" I asked, aloud.

Greatly astonished, I watched as the rock surface shimmered and altered. Was this an illusion? I blinked slowly. No. This was happening, external to myself. This was something new to me.

A large face formed within the stony vortex. It was a wild fierce face, very elemental in its features.

I formed the thought, "Are you an Ancestor?"

The word 'Gate keeper' slipped into my mind in response.

For a while I sat silent, watching to see if something else would happen, unable to think of anything to say. I thought of my axe sitting in my backpack but didn't want to move fearing the face would disappear if I did.

I recalled ancient myths where gatekeepers guard the entrance to other worlds. I sent out the mental question, "Can I come through the gate and meet with the Ancestors?"

The wild face dissolved and in its place a gigantic head appeared which filled the entire area at the end of the cave. The face was that of an Aboriginal man with strong, beautiful features. The expression was peaceful and relaxed. He observed me with glinting eyes, his wide, beautifully sculpted lips half smiling as if he was amused by my astonishment.

I wished I could have thought of deep searching questions to ask but I couldn't think of any. I was completely overawed. All I could think to do was to reach for my notebook and try to draw him. As soon as I started, a gust of wind came from nowhere and blew my page over.

I acknowledged in my thoughts that I understood that he did not want me to draw him. For a long time we just regarded each other until a tourist strolling by entered the cave. Instantly the expression on the face hardened. The eyes shifted to look at the person, and narrowing, became watchful, as if the Being were thinking, "Are you going to behave?" This happened three times. Each time his face relaxed and his eyes returned to regard me as the people left, seemingly unaware of his gigantic presence. How was it that I could see him with my eyes open, when they could not? Had I been able to somehow temporarily tune my physical eyes to a different frequency?

Not sure if I had been right in my interpretation, I summoned up courage and tried once more to draw him but again a gust of wind blew the pages over. There was no sense of offence taken, or anger, just firmness.

Finally I thought to ask. "Who are you?"

Straight away a small green bird flew into the cave and tried to settle on his lips. Unable to perch, it then flew higher and settled on his broad nose. Finally it flew higher still and perched on a rocky ledge I had not noticed until that moment. As I shifted my gaze I saw the bird was sitting on the Being's shoulder and suddenly I saw his arm outstretched protectively along the roof of the cave. In that instant I realized this was the Guardian of the Cave and in the out-flung arm I also saw that he was showing me the way. I understood then that my axe needed to travel further. Uluru was not my place of connection after all.

The instant I got those sudden insights, the face vanished. I sat there lost in thought, all the questions I could have asked suddenly flooding my mind. The idea that a decidedly male presence had allowed himself to be visible to my female eyes in a place regarded by Aborigines as male dominion seemed so unlikely and yet I was sure it had happened. I realized that the axe might have been the reason.

At this point, a member of my group strolled by and I excitedly called him over. Sitting him on the rock, I tried to show him where I had seen the face. I hoped that if he sat quiet, it might return but it didn't. We strained our eyes for about five minutes before giving up and hurrying back to the rendezvous point. Boarding the coach, I suddenly realized that I must have sat there looking at the Being for more than an hour.

****

"...I learned that at sunrise in many parts of the world there is a unique electromagnetic transmission. For twenty minutes the earth along the sun line is blanketed by a wave with a frequency of ten cycles per second. Later this fades and falls back to the three or four cycle hum that forms the constant background to our daily lives...
...Our systems both planetary and personal are governed by the same time keeper."
Lyall Watson - Gifts of Unknown Things

Early next morning, as the last of the stars lost their sparkle in the growing light, we gathered in sleepy silence outside the hotel entrance for the next leg of our journey by coach. Soaking up those wonderful, still moments of sunrise, I gazed across the scrubland, watching as colour tinged with gold came flooding back into the bushes. The soil ignited and burst into flaming red, like Beauty awakened by the caress of a solar prince.

The road to Kings Canyon unravelled like a tarmac ribbon straight across the red dunes, with their covering of mulga and mallee scrubland, for a mesmerizing one hundred and ninety-five miles. There was a video system on the coach and Heather chose this moment as the opportunity to play a recording of the Anangu being given back the ancestral rights to the land. As I watched the 'hand back' ceremony from my seat in the rear of the coach, I felt a strong presence building around me. In an instant I was re-connected with the remarkable, mystical experience of the day before. Certainty swept over me.

I felt sure that now I could draw the Guardian.

My biro pen felt guided as I quickly sketched, and at the finish I was satisfied by the likeness to that beautiful face.

CHAPTER SIXTEEN

*"Aborigines say to white Australians, you are the
ones who are new and inexperienced here.
Carry out the Law the proper way. The significance
of things can only be grasped if you slow down. "*
Aboriginal elder (unknown)

*"...The real thing is listening to everything.
Listening and understanding everything."*
Tjamiwa, Aboriginal elder from Uluru-KataTjuta National Park

*"(White people) only talk politics and study on paper.
But we study...We go in the forest and look carefully.
They don't know our wisdom. It is very different.
White people's knowledge is different - it's all on paper..."*
Spokesman for the Yanomami tribe,
'Kindred Spirit', Summer 2000

It was midday before the coach turned in to
Wanbanalong Station where we were to stay the night.
Our accommodation was simple tent cabins, a contrast
to the grand rooms of Yulara, which, though impressive,
made me feel slightly uncomfortable.

The little tent with its fabric walls filled me with a sense
of pleasure. I always loved being close to the elements.
Later, trailing across to the lavatory building in the dead
of night, I was lost in a magical experience. Standing
shivering in the chilly winter air, I forgot the discomfort
in the wonder of stargazing. The sky was a vast and
crowded star bowl studded with brilliant points of light,
which winked and glittered in the utter silence of the
Outback night.

But that experience was yet to come.

Sitting on a rock in the midday sunshine, I watched a few sorry-looking kangaroos loping around an enclosure. I wondered if they were being kept for dinner or to entertain the passers by.

Beside me, a small lizard scuttled out from a bush and bobbed his head at me before streaking off, his tail leaving a faint wiggling line as evidence of his passing.

I munched my sandwich, enjoying the warmth on my back. The sound of an engine made me turn round in time to see a dusty Range Rover draw to a halt. Through the dirty windscreen I could just make out a familiar figure in a red plaid shirt sitting behind the wheel. N'Dhala. Beaming broadly, she climbed out of the dusty cab and gave me a hug. She seemed more confident, quietly exuding an air of authority. She was on home territory, I realized. This was where she belonged.

I was almost bursting with excitement about what had happened at Uluru. I had so much to tell her but I knew this was not the right moment. I would have to wait.

The coach followed her as she led the way to her tribal homeland. We had only travelled a short distance before the Range Rover turned onto a dusty track that wound its way through the bush. For a mile we bumped through potholes, following the trail of dust until a big sign announced that we had arrived at our destination.

As soon as we arrived, I had a premonition that something special was about to happen. Little flashes of dejas vu started snatching at the edges of my awareness, trying to grab my attention.

N'Dhala was standing there, all smiles, waiting to introduce us to our first real taste of bush culture. At this point I was unaware of her role within the community. It was more than a week later, that looking through my summit directory, I found out that she was one of the traditional owners of the area, which was the ancestral homeland for her people.

She led us single file along a narrow track to a clearing where there was a round wooden building. Filing into the greeting hut, we sat down quietly and looked about. The dusty smell of the tamped-down earth floor, the curved walls and the thick tree trunks supporting the roof in the centre reminded me strongly of the round-house on the Esselen sacred grounds in California.

Understanding was digging its elbow into my consciousness.

Jakamura, a tall and wildly handsome black man strode into the hut. Squatting down on his haunches he began to talk. He spoke of tribal ways, of respect. He talked of his people's relationship to the earth, gradually weaving a spell of words that pulled me into an altered space. Leading us through the bush, he opened our senses to many things. In one place we were encouraged to taste and smell, in another, to be still and listen. Within a cave, he recounted with animated gestures the creation myths of his people and showed us a gallery of their handprints. All the while I found my senses stretching out, invisible antennae reaching in all directions. Something was about to happen. I lay against the smooth white bark of a leaning ghost gum tree and listened to Jakamura, his glossy, black hair tumbling across his face as he explained the symbolism in Aboriginal paintings by drawing examples in the dust with his finger.

We walked in single file as Jakamura led us to a water hole, its still surface reflecting the curving rock face of the cliff above. On the way, we passed more ghost gums leaning over the path.

My memory jolted into wakefulness. I remembered my vision; the drawings and notes I had with me in my suitcase. I began to watch for a dry riverbed and scanned the landscape for the crescent-shaped cliffs.

A short while later, N'Dhala took over from Jakamura. She led the way towards the foot of the cliffs. On the way, we had to negotiate the small but steep drop down a bank in order to cross a dry riverbed. The land began to rise and soon we were scrambling up the side of a steep hill. The rock surface beneath our feet was hazardous, covered with crumbling red stone. All of us, aware of the dangers of slipping, kept our eyes focused on the trail.

The ascent ended abruptly with the rock levelling out onto a flat tableland. As each person in turn arrived at the top, they paused to draw breath and gaze at the view. Absolute stillness filled me when my turn came. The cliffs stretched away, a beautiful red crescent, curving around the bush-covered landscape through which we had walked with Jakamura a short while before. The curve of the cliffs could only be seen from this vantage point. It exactly matched the drawing I made of my vision. Just like N'Dhala, I had seen a clear picture of her homelands in my mind. Quietly I got out my axe and laid it down for a few minutes upon the rock. This was the place to which the axe needed to be connected. From where I was standing I could make out the wise old face within the surface of the axe. I fancied he was smiling.

Before we moved on I took a photograph of the cliffs to compare with my drawing. I needed proof that I was not deluding myself.

"Everything in the field of time and space is dual."
Joseph Campbell

Sure now that I was where I needed to be, I told Jakamura about how I found the stone finger and axe, and about the quest I had embarked on which had led me to their land.

As I related the story I could see enormous surprise on his face. "This is incredible," he said. "This is the story of a film script I was shown last year. It's identical!" He shared with me a story so uncannily like my own journey with the axe that I in turn was greatly surprised.

At this point, N'Dhala arrived. Hearing what had happened, she gasped and her hand flew to her mouth. She had completely forgotten the incident.

"I can't believe I didn't remember this when I heard your story on South Molle!" she exclaimed.

Later she recalled the details.

"They were a Slovenian film company," she said, "and the theme of the film they were shooting went something like this:"

"Someone had a rock that took them on a long journey because they were trying to find where it belonged. In the film the person - the caretaker of the rock - would find their way to a community and realise it was the place. They would then become involved with the people living in the area....the film-makers realised Unity would make the perfect setting for the movie and where to take the rock back to. However we lost contact. We assume all that war stuff got in the way."

Listening, I knew my quest had come to its end. What remained to be answered was why I had been guided there.

CHAPTER SEVENTEEN

"......To know that what is impenetrable really exists,
manifesting itself as the highest wisdom and most
radiant beauty......"
Albert Einstein

If this were a fictional story, everything would be wrapped up at this point- a neat ending about mission accomplished.

However, it is not.

Something happened the following day that was of even greater significance to the journey than the culmination of the quest, something that altered everything I had planned.

A trek through Kings Canyon, guided by Jakamura and N'Dhala, was expected to be one of the highlights of our trip. Australia's 'grand canyon' attracted many tourists and there were other coaches already parked when we arrived. I felt a prick of disappointment at the thought of sharing the canyon with a hundred and one others but this disappeared as we followed Jakamura single file along the heavily wooded, boulder-strewn canyon floor. A powerful river of energy with eddying currents flowed round us as we walked. The feeling of headiness and walking through air pockets should have been a warning to ensure I was properly earthed, but, unusually for me, I was oblivious to the signs, still 'high' with the excitement of what happened the day before. There was no question in my mind about what it signified. I had been led to the community to work with them. But as before when I had made assumptions, Coyote stepped in and took a hand.

We had gone only a short distance into the canyon when Jakamura suddenly left the trail. A short scramble across rocks to the left of the path, I caught a glimpse of water. A dreaming pool. Jakamura squatted down by the water. Curious, I followed him. The surface was treacherous, the scramble difficult. I eased myself on my bottom over the edge of one rock, conscious of the hazards. I remember checking everything so carefully, ensuring a wide enough ledge with no loose stones. As a self-employed therapist, looking after my safety had become a way of life.

Standing up, I dusted myself off, pleased with the precautions I was taking, and spent a moment appreciating the striations in the rocks beside me, beautiful patterns in reds, oranges and ochres.

I still do not know how it happened. I didn't trip, slip or lose my balance. Yet the next thing I knew I was hurtling through the air towards the boulders below. I just managed to get my left hand up to protect my head before impact. I can clearly remember the sense of outraged astonishment and the thought "S...t ! How did this happen?"

As I hit the rocks, my thigh took first impact in a crushing blow. Then my wrist and head hit the rock. The sound of my head on rock was like a shot. I also remember a strange burst of smell and taste on impact.

For a moment I lay stunned, then struggled to sit up, aware of the horrified sounds from others close by as they scrambled down to where I lay. My arm was useless but I was frightened far more by the severe pain that shot through my pelvis as I tried to move. I knew I was in a bad way.

Jakamura scrambled across and placed his hand on my head in concern. Checking first that the others could reach me, he rushed away to get help.

How fortunate I was, being with a group of fellow healers and therapists. Arnica tablets appeared in a trice and were administered every fifteen minutes. Those with me were able to witness the tiny tablets' miraculous effects as a huge bruise bloomed on the side of my face causing it to swell. It blackened and started to disperse almost immediately under their gaze. In less than two hours the bruise was almost gone.

People took turns in supporting me as I propped myself against the rock. The whole group gave me healing and I am sure that without their input, the outcome would have been far more serious.

Waiting for the paramedics, we cracked little jokes, the typical response to situations of this nature. Bea Agins sat opposite me holding my good hand. She teased me gently.

"Little birds need to be sure their wings are strong enough before they try flying," she quipped.

I grinned at her through the pain and closed my eyes. Internally my smile turned wry. How apt. Not for the first time I was being likened to a fallen fledgling.

I thought of a previous fall of a different kind when I had used the same analogy.

Spiritually ambitious at the time, I had been determinedly climbing Jacob's Ladder, my eyes fixed on ethereal planes. When I came to a threshold of choice, I took a leap of faith and left my marriage, confident in the expectation that I would be supported and shielded from the worst of the traumas. The results were not what I had expected. The spiritual fledgling, testing her wings, plummeted to Earth. I felt disconnected and alone with the pain of grief and guilt. The sense of severance from God, of betrayal and abandonment, was appalling, fear and anger my dominating emotions. In spiritual isolation, I worked my way over the next four years through the dark night of the soul, through spiritual death to rebirth, realizing somewhere along the way that I had never been abandoned; that I was not being punished. Rather, I was in the process of discovering and strengthening qualities I did not know I had, owning and working through negative aspects of my nature, things that I needed for the next step of my journey. It was the beginning of my acceptance that I needed to be firmly rooted in human experience in order to bring "Spirit into Matter."

Lying on the rocks I recognized this as another levelling moment for the purpose of growth. Only by having my feet planted solidly on the ground could my dreams for the future find practical application. The deeper implications of this insight I did not see for several months.

Always telling others about the importance of earthing, I had ignored this for myself in the excitement of the last few days. Now, I was being shown in the most forceful way possible that I was un-earthed and out of balance. I had been brought literally down to earth with a bump. Looking at the faces of those around me I knew it had had the same effect on them too.

Fledgling jokes continued to be bandied back and forth until help arrived.

"Gee! Your arm is as crook as an emu's neck!" exclaimed the robust young paramedic as she started her examination. She smiled reassuringly at me, her attractive face unable to conceal concern. There was fear that I had fractured my pelvis too. But they didn't even notice the head injury until we pointed out I had struck rock with the side of my face. The arnica had done a fantastic job!

Getting me out of the canyon on a stretcher was very tricky - a slow, laborious trek. Members of my party took turns helping the paramedics with the stretcher. By this time I had surrendered and was only partially aware of the activity around me but, even so, I was conscious through my haze of the laboured breathing of those struggling to carry me, as they stumbled and slipped across the boulders. Negotiating the track with its narrow twists and turns proved extremely challenging but finally they made it. The flying doctor, we were told, had been called and was standing by.

I gritted my teeth and endured the pain as I was loaded into the neat little plane. One of the group, Pia, accompanied me to the hospital in Alice Springs where I could get proper attention. A specialist in paediatric nursing, it had been her lifelong ambition to fly with the flying doctor. Through half closed eyes I watched her examine the interior of the plane with the eyes of a professional. It was very well equipped with modern technology. All the emergency equipment of a casualty department seemed to be there. I smiled and thought how in every apparent disaster there is a gift. I was content for the moment for the gift to be hers.

Even in the state I was in, I felt a sense of adventure. Flying Doctor! Wow! Another first.

The nightmare of examination and admission to hospital passed in a pethadine blur, and I was only partially conscious of being transferred to the ward. Soft padding footsteps, the whispering swish of uniforms and the gentle hands that took my pulse punctuated my fitful dreams all through the night.

CHAPTER EIGHTEEN

"View your life through eyes filled with humour.
Don't take anything too seriously, least of all yourself!"
Coyote Medicine. Native American wisdom

"My Hands are the tools of my soul."
Navaho

When I woke next morning, the humour of the situation made me laugh out loud. I was in the old children's ward. The dilapidated walls were covered in murals. All around me painted birds flew across treetops or fed fledglings in their nests. Beneath them, emus looking round-eyed and saucy stretched crooknecks to pluck bright red berries. And dominating it all was a large mural of the canyon with a sign saying, "Beware of falling rocks!"

The Universe seemed to be saying, " Don't take any of this too seriously!"

Lying in bed, I was able to observe my three ward companions. A pretty young woman diagonally opposite me was in the process of being admitted. She sat quietly with drooping head on the side of the bed. A white male nurse came and sat beside her and I watched as a touching little scene unfolded. Laying down his clipboard he took her hand and stroked it gently while a whispered conversation took place. Neither looked at the other but as I watched, some of the tension and fear left her face. He sat with her for about ten minutes before he picked up his clipboard and resumed taking details. The nurses and doctors I met during my two-week stay in Alice

Springs Hospital treated the patients with a sensitivity and respect that I found quite remarkable.

Looking round the room, I saw that all the patients apart from myself were Aboriginal people. As the day wore on, I discovered all my companions were those who had returned to their ancestral lands and were living a blend of western and traditional ways in tribal communities. Through the accident, I had gained access to those I had been told it would be impossible to meet. As a result, my time in hospital was to become a most significant and valued part of the trip to Australia. I was being given the opportunity to make friends with those who still practised, to a certain extent, the hunter-gatherer ways of their ancestors.

Directly opposite me, was a woman with legs swathed in bandages. Her interaction and rapport with staff indicated she had been there for some time. Like many Aboriginal people she had a chronic chest infection and diabetes, the insidious diseases caused by contact with Western Civilization. Her strong features split into a ready smile when she talked to the nurses. Several times I tried to attract her attention. I called a greeting but she ignored me. I thought I was experiencing the hostility shown towards white people about which I had been warned. But I was wrong. It wasn't that at all. She surprised me suddenly by catching my eye and smiling.

Annette became a close companion. Aboriginal people, who are very reticent, normally speak in very low whispers when they are unsure of themselves. Annette, I discovered, was slightly deaf. She had not heard me when I called. Because of her deafness she spoke louder and relied on more eye contact than usual, which made it easier for me to befriend her.

The hospital experience has a wonderful way of lowering barriers and developing intimacy between people. Our common problems made it easier for us to develop a friendship not hampered by reserve. Annette quickly found that I was genuinely interested in her as a person. Talking to her was endlessly fascinating. For information on everyday activities in a modern tribal community, I could not have had a better teacher. I discovered with surprise that she was a film buff. She was far better informed about recent video releases than I and seemed to have watched them all. However, one film above all others remained her favourite - "Geronimo". I suspected this was because she identified with the story of an oppressed people fighting for their land.

She told me with satisfaction that her husband's last hunt had been especially successful and her freezer was full of kangaroo meat. As we talked, I began to get a picture of a community that takes what suits it from the modern technological world while retaining ancestral practices.

She was a natural teacher, direct in manner and rather dogmatic, but nevertheless an entertaining companion. At the slightest prompting, she would instruct me in various aspects of 'women's business'. I learned a lot from her about 'skin names', a system which divides the tribal population into categories. She told me how belonging to a certain 'skin' imposed certain rules of behaviour and defined whom one could marry and with whom one could associate. It was almost like a subsection within the tribe.

She talked a lot about 'sorry business', how Aboriginal people are very 'strong' about emotional health. They felt tragedy very keenly.

"When someone dies, that is 'sorry business'. People stop everything. They go to 'sorry camp' for one week," she explained. At the camp the mourners gave full vent to their grief.

"They've got to get it out," she said. "Then they become healthy again."

During 'sorry business', those mourning do not speak. Instead they have a finely developed sign language through which to communicate. This same sign language is commonly used when communicating with another 'mob'. I learned that she could not speak the same language as the two other ward companions. Far from ignoring each other as I had supposed, I learned that they were communicating through subtle signs.

"There are so many languages here," she said. "English is not my first language. Maybe it's my number three language." I thought humbly about my total lack of language skills and vowed to change this on my return home.

When a person dies their name becomes taboo for a period of time. It is a sign of respect for the dead person. It causes quite a predicament when several living people share the same name. Annette's aunt of the same name had died and for a time Annette had been referred to by the universal name of Kumunjayi or by her initials A.J. "It can cause a lot of mix up," she said. She paused, popping a wad of chewing tobacco in her mouth while she thought about what else she could tell me.

I had noticed a small ceremony take place every time Annette had a visitor. A piece of silver paper was taken out of her drawer and opened. Into it were placed small pieces of chewing tobacco from her guests. I presumed it was an Aboriginal bedside gift equivalent to grapes or flowers.

Continuing, she said, "A lady called Alice died here. She was really respected. So we call here, Kumunjayi Springs." Her dark face split into a wide grin when she saw me writing things down, displaying teeth temporarily stained yellow with tobacco juice. She stabbed at my paper with her forefinger.

"You put down that my grandfather is ninety-nine years old."

I discovered then that her grandfather had been instrumental in fighting for land rights for the Warlpiri. It took them until the seventies before they could reclaim their land. Now the most ancient of all the elders, he still passes on tribal tradition and teaches The Law.

Sitting in bed one afternoon early on in our association, she regaled me with accounts of goanna and kangaroo hunts. She waved a bandaged foot at me. "I cut my foot on a goanna hunt, running after a goanna through the spinifex grass." Being diabetic, she was prone to infection. The cuts had ulcerated and she now needed skin grafts. She bore it all stoically.

She also touched briefly on food taboos; which foods were forbidden to certain groups of people and which ones were special favourites. Kangaroo heads and tails were taboo food for everyone except old people. Goanna (a lizard) tasted like chicken and was a particular favourite of children. "It is small and it is difficult to share around a lot of people." I learned that the Aborigine share everything.

She told me about collecting 'bush tucker' and described which plants were eaten when ill, to give strength or to stave off hunger. There were also plants to make you dream well.

Perhaps the most surprising conversation we had was when she spoke of visits by UFOs.

"What are they like?" I asked.

"Lots of pretty colours. Colours playing all around," she said.

When I asked her why she thought they came, she was silent for a while. Eventually she volunteered, "I think they come for water."

"Why?" I asked.

"Because the ground and the bush is much drier where they have been."

You would have to be Aboriginal to discern something like that in such an arid area.

Annette's parting gift to me was a dot painting of her grandmother's dreaming - 'Ngurlu dreaming' - women collecting 'bush tucker'. Each dot, each wavy line told of the trails through the bush in search of roots and seeds. Each cluster of horseshoe shapes described the sorting and sifting and preparation of the food during which the women told each other stories. I watched her as she sat beside her bed patiently working away for hours until she finished. I later discovered she did not like painting so it really was a labour of love. People have told me since that I am indeed honoured. Aboriginal people do not give gifts lightly to white folks. Months passed without news following my return. Then finally a letter dropped through my letterbox. At the very moment it came, I was sitting beneath Annette's dot painting in my kitchen, talking to Ibrahim Abu el Hawa, a small, dynamic Palestinian who works for peaceful co-existence between Muslim and Jew in The Holy Land. A stateless person, he had just described himself as an Aborigine of the Middle East and, prompted by this, I embarked upon the tale of my journey and my meeting with Annette. I had just finished an explanation of the symbolic meaning of her picture when I heard the sound of the letterbox flap. Wondering wistfully out loud how she was and how I wished she would write, I went for the post.

There was just the one letter - an airmail.

It was from Annette, wondering in turn how I was and wishing for news of me. I was stunned by the extraordinary synchronicity. Opposite Ibrahim sat with a quizzical expression on his face, his kindly eyes watching me through pebble-thick glasses as I read Annette's letter. Her final paragraph touched me so deeply and I burst into loud sobs. It was a few minutes before I had breath enough to explain to Ibrahim, rocking me now in his arms in fatherly concern, that I wasn't unhappy. In truth I was ecstatic. Annette had asked me to take her 'skin' name so that we could be 'skin sisters'.

Kirsten 'Nabangardi' Bolwig.

In that moment I felt honoured beyond measure. Every time I look at the painting now I feel the connection between us and feel a great sense of privilege.

Shortly after returning from Australia I received a book from N'Dhala by anthropologist Diane Bell. Annette had urged me to read it. Through it my knowledge about the Warlpiri tribe has continued to deepen. The book, called "Daughters of the Dreaming", is a vivid account of anthropologist Diane Bell's friendship with the women of Ali Curung, including Annette's grandmother, mother and aunt.

CHAPTER NINETEEN

"The Yanomami already looked after this earth long before any politicians arrived. Our communities don't have paper. Our 'paper' is our thoughts, our beliefs. Our 'paper' is very ancient; we had it long before white people arrived...."
Spokesman for the Yanomami tribe, 'Kindred Spirit', Summer 2000

Propped up in the hospital bed, I finally had the time to leaf through the Australian Healing Summit 2000 directory. I discovered on reading N'Dhala's short biography that she was a Traditional Owner of the land where the people of Unity lived. She was seeking to build interracial harmony using spirituality as the means, highlighting the fact that there are spiritual principles universal to all religions.

Together with a small group she had set up a co-operative business venture, an Aboriginal tour company, to provide income for her mob. Through the guided walks, Jakamura and the other guides had an opportunity to stimulate awareness of existence extending beyond the physical realm. Even the short excursion provided for our party at Unity had the effect of stretching the physical senses into more subtle dimensions. Walking through the bush with its encircling backdrop of vibrant red cliffs, it was impossible not to become conscious of the planet being a living entity or have a sense of ancient spiritual beings still active and influencing the present. It engendered respect.

Over and over again, I have heard the word 'respect' being used in the place of 'love' by both the Aboriginal people and the Native Americans I had encountered, and in the correct usage of the word, I have come to realize that this quality more clearly defines what humanity should be striving towards, for implicit in its energy is the Love that is referred to by people without real comprehension of its nature.

Lying back against my pillows I closed my eyes and thought about the recent surge of interest in hunter-gatherer groups and their perspectives. If there were a union between earth-wisdom and modern scientific thought, it would provide us with the understanding and the knowledge to move forward through what Gregg Braden calls "this unprecedented time in history".

****

As N'Dhala walked into the ward for the first time, I wept with delight, realizing as I clung to her hand, how much I had wanted the contact. Through all that had happened, N'Dhala and Jakamura had suddenly taken on a position of huge significance to me.

With her she brought a bunch of beautiful desert flowers, many of them the same as those that had entranced me at Uluru. She had chosen with care, picking a collection of soft colours. There were mauves, lilacs, creams and silvers, interspersed with the jolly yellow and white 'poached egg' blooms of an everlasting daisy. The pastel shades, reviving the memory of the flowers at Uluru, gave me pleasure throughout my two-week stay in hospital. Not even the standard hospital vase, a jam jar, could detract from their beauty.

Sitting down, N'Dhala took my plastered hand in hers, and quietly closed her eyes. For several minutes we sat in silence, while I felt the flow of healing energy she channelled travel up my arm and round my battered body; felt the shock in my system gradually draining away. All the damage sites were bathed in warmth more comforting than from any heat lamp.

It occurred to me that in my passion to help heal the fractures between the black and white people of Australia, I had allowed myself to become too subjective, a state in which no healer or therapist can afford to be. With sudden insight I wondered if, in some part, my own fractures were an empathic representation of those I wished to heal. Perhaps I had known, deep down, that my time in the country would be too limited to be useful. I could not stay to heal the wound so I was taking it back as homework. To me, as I lay there, it seemed plausible. What an idiot if it were so!

N'dhala opened her eyes and glanced around. No one appeared to be taking any interest in what she did. Life in the ward went on as usual. The tea trolley came and went. Hospital routine is essentially the same wherever you are in the world, it seems. As I sipped tea out of a polystyrene cup, we talked of my accident.

"When you come into areas like that you can be affected on levels you don't even recognize immediately." she said.

I remembered something Heather had said about three circles etched into the surface of the rock by the pool and an energy connection with Unity. Perhaps I had got caught up in an energy current strong enough to push me over the edge of the rock.

N'Dhala became a frequent visitor at my bedside. Living as she did on the outskirts of Alice Springs, she could pop in as she chose. Through the accident, I had been given the gift of two precious weeks in which to get to know her. I was aware of a bond between us that sprang from an intangible source deeper than mere friendship.

She would sit on the edge of the bed speaking quietly in the manner of the Aboriginal people. She was a delightful, humorous companion, an immensely sensitive person, and the time we shared sped by. Deep in conversation, we explored beliefs, shared insights and ideas, hopes and dreams. We both wanted cross-cultural fertilization as a way to build respect and heal the wounds caused by racialism. I realized that, interested in spiritual growth as she was, and being of mixed race, she had a foot in both camps. It was possible for her to draw on the spiritual wisdom of both. I could see the potential for the two spiritual heritages to be integrated through her, both for her own benefit and that of others.

During one of her visits N'Dhala showed me pictures of Unity and I was able to get glimpses of a community in the process of development as, one by one, members of her mob were traced and offered the opportunity to return home. There were pictures of Jakamura and his adult son, side-by-side, poring in earnest concentration over business plans. Looking at the photographs, I regretted the lack of opportunity to get to know him. I wondered again about the two parallel stories of stone quests homing in on Unity. It was Jakamura who had seen the connection. Only time would reveal if anything could develop from the meeting.

Everything N'Dhala told me was interesting but her account of her social work with Aborigines struggling against alcoholism and addiction was also deeply saddening. Rootless, aimless, without their Ancestral Law to provide structure for their lives, many urban Aborigines have turned to drink and drugs to dull the pain. Understaffed and under funded, N'Dhala and other social workers made little headway in their battle against the hopelessness and fecklessness of their Aboriginal clients.

To lift my mood she described the wonder of sleeping under the stars, how on cold nights the Unity dogs shared her swag. "All their warm bodies snuggling round me, keeping me warm. Last time I slept out at Unity it was a four-dog night. Quite cold."

I realized that she gauged the chill of the night by the number of dogs that snuggled up to her. I pictured the warm huddle sharing her swag and thought of my own longing to sleep under the stars at Uluru.

****

"If a man does not keep pace with his companions, perhaps it is because he hears a different drummer. Let him step in time with the music that he hears."
Edmund James Banfield "The Beachcomber"

Touching on similarities between beliefs, I learned with particular interest how Aboriginal people are able to see that the message is intrinsically the same whatever the religion. Many Aboriginal people have been able to adopt Christ's teachings and live them much more readily than some cultures that have supposedly had these teachings for centuries. They see no conflict between Aboriginal Spiritual Law and Christianity because to them Jesus is a Law Man in the spiritual sense of the word.

It is sad that Aboriginal people are expansive enough in their thinking to accept the Christian Son of God, yet most Christians would neither recognize nor respect the wisdom they have to offer in return.

In one particular community, she told me, women educated as Catholic still practised their Law. They decided that God had made the Dreaming for Aboriginal people, coming to this conclusion even though the early missionaries had forbidden their cultural and spiritual activities. It seemed Aboriginal people have been able to separate out the real message of Jesus from the actions of so-called Christians and the damage they did to Aboriginal culture. If people everywhere could adopt this stance, all the wars that have been started on the grounds of religious or spiritual beliefs would not happen. They would see past religious interpretation and ritual, and look deeper into the universal message - Love and Peace on Earth.

N'Dhala also shared with me something that I found particularly interesting.

In a community where there has been no missionary influence, there is a group of senior Aboriginal women who still live the Law and who only refer to Jesus as Kwemantjay (I realized that she must be referring to what Annette had called 'Kumunjayi'). To show respect, the term is used instead of a dead person's name. The length of time it is used depends on the importance of the person and how deeply people were affected by their passing. It can range from a few months to a number of years. In the case of Jesus, these women feel so much respect for him that they still won't say his name although it is 2000 years since his passing. They even refer to Christmas holidays as 'Kwemantjay holidays'.

I felt humbled by this mark of respect.

****

I was making fast progress in my healing. My wrist, mangled and shattered and likened to "a digestive biscuit that has been trod on", needed four attempts to set it, including two operations. But my hip, although having massive impact crush injury, was not broken. Slowly I began to improve in mobility with the aid of a zimmer frame. How wonderfully safe I felt leaning on its metal structure. How panic-stricken when they took it away and gave me a crutch instead.

In the middle of my second week N'Dhala came in pushing a wheel chair. "How about we go out for lunch?" She suggested. The Great Escape! The feeling of fresh air once again on my face was wonderful. I tilted my face into the sun enjoying the warmth as I was pushed along. In the distance the red slopes of The West MacDonnell Ranges formed a dramatic backdrop to Alice Springs.

The Mall, Alice's main pedestrian street, looked almost Mediterranean with its tall eucalyptus trees casting welcome shade over pavement cafes. The illusion was dispelled when, sitting beneath a tree, waiting while N'Dhala went into a shop, I felt the familiar rain of leaves and twigs upon my head. I knew without looking up that there was a parrot feeding overhead. People sauntered down the street, stopped and talked. No rush. No worries. Evidence all around of a laid back approach to life.

At a table, crammed alongside others in a covered alley outside a delicatessen, we shared a dish of Aussie proportions. My stomach, used to hospital size portions, could not cope with the quantity and before long I abandoned any attempts to eat more. The whole affair was punctuated with interruptions. Several times in the process of eating, N'Dhala had to stop to retrieve my crutch as it slid with a clatter beneath the table, or move the wheel chair closer to my plate as people squeezed past on their way to and fro. As irritating as it might have been for her, it was wonderful for me. I gloried in being part of the noisy hubbub of humanity once again.

She glanced up from sipping her cappuccino and smiled as someone greeted her in passing. I watched her as she took another sip, another spoonful and waved at yet another person. She was obviously well known and liked. Several times as she wheeled me along the street, we had paused to exchange greetings with others.

I had noticed her coughing from time to time.

"Are you O.K.?" I eventually asked, slightly anxious. She brushed it aside. Just a slight chest infection she assured me.

I relaxed then and in a happy haze listened to her soft voice with its rising cadence at the end of each sentence, telling me of her hopes and dreams. But a short while later I realized N'Dhala was coughing more and more frequently as once again she pushed me from shop to shop. Becoming concerned, I twisted round and looked at her. Two hectic spots of colour stained her cheeks a darker red. Her eyes glittered. I could see she was not well. Feeling contrite at not realizing her condition before, thinking of all the talking she had done, I insisted on taking a taxi back to the hospital. She gave in without protest. I did not see her again until the day before I left.

****

"I am a red man. If the Great Spirit had wanted me to be a white man he would have made me so in the first place. He put in your hearts certain wishes and plans, in my heart he put other and different desires. Each man is good in his sight. It is not necessary for eagles to be crows."
Tatanka Yotanka (Sitting Bull) Hunkpapa Sioux Chief 1877

N'Dhala's final visit to the hospital passed with the reserve that overtakes people just before parting. We had so much still to share and no more time. The end came in a rush of last minute changes. My flight was pushed forward by several hours. N'Dhala met me at the airport, bringing with her a film I had requested so that I was able to take a photograph, the only picture of her that I have. I caught a final glimpse of her waving to me from the crowd as I was pushed towards the doors of the departure lounge.

As the giant plane winged its way over the curving surface of our planetary jewel, I was riveted again by the series of stunningly beautiful, naturally repeating patterns in the Australian landscape as it slid by beneath us. Even thousands of feet above the ground as I was, I felt the power of the land and loved it.

Moved by the rolling display of natural art, I reached into my hand luggage and took out the axe-head. I cradled it between my hands feeling the cool smoothness of its polished surface, appreciating the contrasting elements used to make up its perfect form.

My train of thought shifted to the Aboriginal friends I had made and to the enjoyment of lively discussions which passed the time from one meal to another. For all we had in common, it came to light that they nevertheless viewed many things from a different perspective.

When N'Dhala learned of my dreams for helping her community, she made me realize that, at present, what the people of Unity need is the space to re-form themselves as a tribe and the time to heal their own psychological wounds without contributions or interference from outsiders – at least, not for the time being. The realization of this was accompanied by a huge sense disappointment even as I was forced to accept it.

Listening to both women talk about their communities I came to realize that amongst many Aborigines (as with indigenous people elsewhere) there is a wish to retain separateness, fearing a loss of their own uniqueness. I remembered also the brief moment at the conference of friction between 'Auntie' and the organizers over the observance of courtesies. Interested in working towards interracial harmony as I am, the importance of exercising respect for different perspectives really struck home.

It is strange and sad how down through the ages events have shown Mankind to be intolerant of diversity. Throughout history, civilizations have sought to override or destroy other the cultures with which they have come into contact.

A belief crystallized within me for which the axe was a perfect metaphor with its different elements combining to form a beautiful whole. The way forward for Mankind now is to find union in diversity, and to use the diversity to find creative solutions.

CHAPTER TWENTY

*"We all walk the trails of life by taking one step after
another. How we move is in our hands....*

*I am free to walk in fear or love, to protect myself
or to learn, to travel lightly or carry a heavy load.
How easy it is to forget that guilt is heavy, anger is a burden,
and hate and envy sap the body.*

*How slow I am to understand that laughter is light,
love is freeing, and trust enlightens us."*
'Song of the Circle' Barry Brailsford

At peace, with time to absorb all that had occurred for me
on both physical and spiritual levels, I had plenty of
opportunity to reflect on the multiple layers of the
experience. In the solitude of my Bath home, I came at last
to understand one of the key lessons implicit in my fall.

I realized with a jolt that, somewhere along the way, I
had lost my rose-coloured spectacles. The time in
hospital enabled me to let go of any remnant of old
romantic 'noble savage' notions I still harboured
unconsciously. Coyote, my constant companion, had
helped me get my feet back on the ground and my head
out of the clouds.

A new perspective began to emerge. While I retained my
vision of humanity coming into wholeness, the realization
dawned that I had to become far more down to earth
and realistic if I wished to move my dreams into reality.

_e and reform, both within myself and in the world
.arge, cannot take place if surrounded by illusion.

The way forward was to take all the principles and
spiritual insights that I had learned over twenty-five years
and become involved in all the areas from which I had
spent so many years disassociating myself, including the
socio-economic and political arenas. I rolled up my
metaphorical sleeves and prepared to do some
spadework as a foundation for the future.

But these realizations do not explain why I was led by a
trail of synchronicity and vision to the far side of the
world. The significance of that remains a mystery yet to
be solved.

Like iron filings to a magnet, I was drawn to Unity, where
members of the lost generation of a tribe are being
retrieved and integrated back into the whole. In the
process they are learning to respect, value and work
with the gifts of each individual as they move in truth
towards unity. In their journey I can see my own - my
quest for personal wholeness. I too am in the process of
coming home - to myself - discovering along the way
fragments of myself that need to be accepted and
integrated whilst learning to live and feel comfortable
with the paradox in all things.

Above all else I have learned to trust. Trust the process
no matter where it takes me. Be open for all that is yet
to come. Trust that when the time is right I will
understand.

****

Now that the healing is largely over - physical and emotional - I look at the stone axe, this beautiful symbol of wholeness. No longer is it white one side and dark on the other, having returned to its natural state of uniform colouring. I remain aware that there is yet more to unfold - insights connected to this time of change. I recall Carlo's words, "When the axe is taken home, memories locked within its crystal structure will be released. It is then you will truly know the knowledge it contains."

There is some disagreement about its origin. Examining its surface structure in a preliminary examination, geologists at Bristol University say there is a possibility its origin is outside this country. Archaeologists are unsure. As its present caretaker, one of the things I need to do is find out where it comes from and take it home. Only then will the deeper wisdom of this ancient record keeper be unlocked and further insights be revealed.

> *"I am part of all that I have met;*
> *Yet all experience is an arch wherethro'*
> *Gleams that untravelled world, whose margin fades*
> *For ever and for ever when I move."*
> Alfred Lord Tennyson

Kirsten Bolwig comes from a background of science, open spirituality and human rights activism. Describing herself as a spiritual activist, the focus of her spirituality expresses itself in the understanding that today it is no longer appropriate to limit spirituality to contemplation  and meditation alone. It needs to be synonymous with action and with the application of spiritual insights, understandings and principles in all areas of life.

Her focus today is on raising awareness about the need for harmony in relation to the way in which we live with nature, between each other, and most importantly, within ourselves, the only bit of Mother Earth for which we are truly caretakers.

She has a strong interest in bringing people of Western culture together with those of ancient traditions as the way to foster deeper spiritual, ecological and collective awareness, seeing this as key to creating a more harmonious future of peace and balance.

Working as a transformational healer and complementary therapist in Bath, England, she views everything in all its diversity as an integral part of the Whole.

Also from StarDrum Books......

Cléa and the Fifth Dimension by Esmé Ellis

A prophetic adventure, weaving present-day reality with an expanded future reality in which Cléa, the central character, forms the bridge between the two. In this vision of a new world of extraordinary powers which we are about to enter, death and ageing, as we know them, cease to exist; today's obsession with techno-wizardry is left behind as instantaneous communication/transport systems become the norm. While contemporary characters, Cass and Geoff, develop a supersensory awareness which challenges the narrow scientific views of their colleagues, dream-like glimpses into past and future gel for them into a discovery of personal life-shifting potential. Simultaneously, the reality in which Cléa exists, peopled with Archetypal forces, moves dramatically into our Now. The two stories gradually weave together as they move towards the Eternal Moment where past and future converge, and where we are freed from the limitations of time.

A mysterious blue light, Astrazzurra, illumines and guides the two worlds towards this convergence. But the outcome is far from assured. The terrifying Dark Lord of

Nature rises up to engulf Cléa in the heavy coils of her own past-life degradation. Can she surmount the challenge which involves facing the ultimate horror and fear; an act that will trigger the quantum leap, taking Earth into the Fifth Dimension?

Esmé Ellis trained as a sculptor, first in Sheffield, where she was born and later at the Royal College of Art, London. Her chosen career was tragically snatched away when she succumbed to an acutely painful and paralysing disease in 1981. Rather than the disaster it at first seemed, the illness became a turning point when a miracle occurred. A blue light appeared and began to communicate and heal her. This story is told in her book, PATHWAY INTO SUNRISE, (published by Horus Books in 1998.) She now lives in Bath, where her sculptor's chisel has mutated into a writer's quill. Esmé has recently led workshops and lectured on aspects of spiritual and psychological development. She is also a healer, counsellor and channel for her spiritual guide, Astrazzurra.